D1000523

Coping with

ULCERS, HEARTBURN, AND STRESS-RELATED STOMACH DISORDERS

Judy Monroe

THE ROSEN PUBLISHING GROUP, INC./NEW YORK

Published in 2000 by The Rosen Publishing Group, Inc.
29 East 21st Street, New York, NY 10010

Copyright © 2000 by Judy Monroe

All rights reserved. No part of this book may be reproduced in any form
without permission in writing from the publisher, except by a reviewer.

First Edition

Library of Congress Cataloging-in-Publication Data

Monroe, Judy
     Coping with uclers, heartburn, and stress-related stomach disorders /
by Judy Monroe
     p.   cm. — (Coping)
     Includes bibliographical references and index.
     Summary: Provides information on the most common maladies and
disorders of the stomach and digestive system, with an emphasis on
prevention and early detection.
     ISBN 0-8239-2971-X
     1. Indigestion Juvenile literature. 2. Peptic ulcer Juvenile literature.
[1. Indigestion. 2. Peptic ulcer. 3. Digestive system.] I. Title. II. Title:
Ulcers, heartburn, and stomach-related stress. III. Series: Coping with
series (New York, N.Y.)
RC827.M66 2000
616.3'32—dc21   99-40863
                                                                          CIP

Manufactured in the United States of America

About the Author

Judy Monroe, M.A., M.P.H., has written numerous books and magazine articles for teens on health issues.

Contents

1 Start Thinking About Your Stomach   1

2 Common Stomach Problems   11

3 Heartburn and Beyond   35

4 Peptic Ulcers: The Good News   51

5 Food Intolerances   61

6 The Uncommon Food Allergy   83

7 Take Time to Digest   99

8 Keeping Fit   112

9 Managing Stress   123

Glossary   138

Where to Go for Help   145

For Further Reading   147

Index   150

Start Thinking About Your Stomach

Gwen glanced at her note cards. "Oh, oh," she whispered as she stared at the blue inky smudges that had sweated onto her fingers. Worse, she felt a vague queasiness stir in her stomach. Why did she get so nervous just thinking about being in front of a group of people? After all, she knew everyone in her American history class.

She looked at Duane standing near the blackboard. He seemed relaxed as he talked about a young woman who had dressed as a man to fight in the Civil War. But Gwen couldn't listen for long. She started to go through her notes again.

"Thank you, Duane," she heard Mr. Landy say. Then he motioned to Gwen. "You're next."

That's when Gwen's queasy stomach began to gurgle and moan. Oh, no! She tasted a sour bubble coming up into her throat. How could she talk when she felt like running for the bathroom? Somehow Gwen slowly made her way to the front of the class.

Tummy Turmoil

Like Gwen, many people experience tummy turmoil. This problem happens only occasionally for some. For others, however, their stomach problems happen over and over, sometimes when they are stressed or feeling nervous.

People usually think about their stomach only in terms of "I'm hungry!" or "Is my stomach getting larger, or are my jeans shrinking?" Yet this large, powerful organ performs several important automatic tasks every day.

Most of the time, the stomach does its job efficiently without your being aware of its hard work. At other times problems arise. Stomach problems can range from a queasy, noisy stomach like Gwen's to an occasional bout of diarrhea. But sometimes the symptoms are more serious and ongoing, which could signal a digestive disease. Digestive diseases range from an occasional upset stomach or nausea to stomach cancer or ulcers. An ulcer is a sore on the stomach lining.

Whatever the cause, an upset stomach, sometimes accompanied by nausea or vomiting, is nasty. Upset stomachs caused by motion, too much food, or stress may respond to various helpers—simple stress reducers like taking a deep breath or over-the-counter (OTC) medicines. People can buy OTC medicines without a doctor's prescription, or written instructions. For other stomach woes, professional care is the best course of action.

You're Not Alone

If you sometimes get an upset stomach or indigestion, have an ulcer, or experience other digestive upsets, you are not alone. According to the National Institutes of Health, more than 95 million people in the United States experience some type of digestive problem. Digestion is the process of breaking down food into simpler compounds so that they can be absorbed by the stomach and small intestine.

The cost of all these health problems is staggering. Each year, more than 10 million Americans are hospitalized for their digestive problems. In fact, more Americans are hospitalized for digestive diseases than for any other type of illness. All together, the cost of digestive problems amounts to more than $91 billion each year in terms of doctor visits, hospital stays, lost school and work days, and early deaths. The bottom line: Digestive diseases greatly impact millions and millions of Americans.

Prescription medicines, surgery, or other treatments sometimes can help those with serious digestive diseases. Unfortunately we waste a great deal of money in treating many digestive problems that are not life-threatening. Peek inside the homes of people across the country and you'll find many who squirrel away an assortment of OTC medicines—liquids, pills, tablets, powders, or capsules—to treat heartburn, indigestion, or an upset stomach. Indigestion occurs when the body does not break down foods properly. Yet people who experience occasional stomach problems often can head them off by following simple lifestyle habits that help keep their digestive system healthy.

Common Stomach Problems

Some digestive problems become more common as people get older. However, most can occur at any age, even in children and infants. Anyone is susceptible to developing a digestive problem regardless of their gender, ethnic background, or economic situation.

Problems of the digestive system, also called the gastrointestinal (GI) system, are quite common. Most of us, young and old, have had a stomach upset. You may have had nausea, vomiting, or diarrhea (ongoing runny or watery feces). Sometimes stomach upsets are caused by having the flu or eating too much food. But for others, stomach problems are associated with a digestive disease. Here is an overview of the most common stomach problems:

☞ Heartburn, or Gastroesophageal Reflux Disease (GERD): GERD, or heartburn as it is commonly called, is the backward flow of stomach acid into the esophagus and sometimes the mouth. According to the National Institute of Diabetes and Digestive and Kidney Diseases in Bethesda, Maryland, more than 60 million Americans experience heartburn at least once a month. Of these, more than 25 million suffer heartburn every day.

☞ Ulcers: About 25 million Americans suffer from ulcers, which are sores in the lining of the stomach or small intestine.

☞ Constipation/Diarrhea: "Constipation" is a term used to describe a condition in which people have difficulty moving their bowels, which is the part of the intestine responsible for excretion. The stools are usually dry and hard. In contrast, diarrhea is watery feces expelled frequently. Diarrhea can be deadly. It is the third leading cause of death worldwide, usually hitting the elderly and children the hardest.

4

↪Irritable Bowel Syndrome (IBS): IBS varies among individuals, but typical symptoms include stomach pain, bloating, constipation, and diarrhea. Some people alternate between constipation and diarrhea. IBS is common, occurring in up to 20 percent of Americans.

↪Food Intolerances: A person can have an intolerance, or unpleasant symptoms or reactions, to particular foods. The most common source of problems are foods that contain sugars.

↪Gas: All of us have gas in the stomach or the intestines. However, some people have an excess amount of gas, which can be uncomfortable and sometimes embarrassing if the gas is expelled inappropriately.

↪Gastritis: Gastritis is inflammation of the mucous membrane that lines the stomach. Symptoms include vomiting, stomach cramps, and pain.

Your Digestive System

Your digestive system functions somewhat like a food processor. It metabolizes—digests, breaks down, converts—food into nutrients, which are basically the fuel that your body runs on. These nutrients provide your body with energy. The digestive system also removes unused matter from the body. To better understand how stomach problems arise, here's an overview of your digestive system—a system essential to life.

The Stomach Is Connected to the . . .

The digestive system is a series of hollow organs joined by a long, twisting tube from the mouth to the anus. Inside this tube is a lining called the mucosa. The mucosa contains tiny glands that produce juices to help digest food. The total length of the digestive system runs twenty to thirty feet (about six to nine meters), depending on the age and size of the person.

All digestion of food and water takes place in your GI system, which includes the mouth, esophagus, stomach, small intestine, large intestine, and anus. The mouth, tongue, and teeth make the first contact with any food or beverage you consume. Your mouth and teeth break food into smaller pieces, preparing it to be swallowed.

Once you swallow, food is forced into the pharynx, or throat. From there it goes into the esophagus. This muscular tube, about ten inches (twenty-five centimeters) long, extends nearly straight down into the stomach. A series of muscular contractions called peristalsis moves food through the esophagus and into the stomach. From the moment you swallow a bite of food, it takes about nine seconds to move from the back of the throat through the esophagus.

A circular sphincter muscle at the stomach's entrance is usually tightly shut, but when food arrives, it opens to allow the food to move from the esophagus into the stomach. Then this muscle contracts, closing the opening between the stomach and esophagus. This sphincter muscle acts as a gate—it lets in food but keeps stomach juices from washing back up into the esophagus.

The empty stomach looks somewhat like a J-shaped sack surrounded by three layers of muscles, which stretch to hold a meal. As food enters the stomach, it bulges out into the shape of a boxing glove. The three layers of muscle contract rhythmically, churning food and stomach juices together, around and around, about every twenty seconds. The stomach handles three main activities:

- ➮ It mixes food and gastric, or stomach, juices together. This hastens the breakdown of food and liquids.

- ➮ It holds food temporarily until it is passed into the small intestine.

- ➮ It controls the rate at which food enters the small intestine.

Food stays in your stomach for three to six hours. The rate at which the stomach processes and empties food varies. Liquids pass through fast but solids remain until they are mixed thoroughly with gastric juices. Gastric juices, which are produced by special cells in the stomach lining, are a mixture of hydrochloric acid, digestive enzymes, and mucus. A layer of mucus protects the stomach lining, preventing the gastric juices from damaging the stomach.

The small intestine handles most food absorption into the bloodstream. The small intestine measures about twenty feet (six meters), but it takes up less space than you would think because it is coiled up inside your abdomen. The small intestine is connected to the large intestine, or colon. This five- to six-foot (1.5 to 1.8 meters) muscular tube absorbs water and packages undigested food as feces, or solid waste, which is eliminated through the anus. Solid waste usually remains in the colon a day or two.

How It Works

From the first to last bite of an apple, your digestive system turns this fruit into simpler substances that your body can use. Digestion is a two-fold process: mechanical and chemical. The mechanical part is when you chew, mash, and break food into smaller pieces. The chemical part involves changing the apple into simpler substances by digestive enzymes and stomach acids. Digestive enzymes are proteins that speed up the breakdown of food.

After the apple is digested, it goes through an absorption process in which it moves from the digestive tract into your bloodstream. Blood cells carry the small particles, or molecules of nutrients, to cells throughout your body. In the meantime, any part of the apple that is undigested is eliminated as feces.

Your Amazing Stomach

Care for some more fun facts? Try these:

- ↪ On average your stomach can hold a little more than one quart (0.9 liters) of food.

- ↪ The hydrochloric acid in your stomach is strong enough to dissolve substances made out of metal, such as nails or even razor blades.

- Most bacteria on or in food is destroyed by the hydrochloric acid in your stomach.

- The walls of your stomach contain small pressure sensors that tell the body when the stomach is empty—then you feel hungry.

- The lining of the stomach is digestible by the gastric juices. However, the stomach's mucosa, or mucous coating, is renewed more rapidly than it is removed.

- The mucus produced by your stomach protects your stomach from digesting itself.

- Every three days, your stomach lining is entirely replaced.

What You Will Find in This Book

Most of us take our digestive system for granted because it reliably and efficiently handles what we eat and drink. Each apple or hamburger adds up; the average person eats about half a ton—that's 1,000 pounds—of food a year. After each meal or snack, your digestive system is busy digesting and absorbing food, then eliminating unused material. You seldom need to think about or help out the digestive process. However, many common problems related to this complex system can arise. Most are temporary and are not serious. Some, though, may continue for a period of time, which may indicate a problem that needs the care of a doctor.

The first part of this book covers common stomach problems. Some of these are related to eating habits and the kinds of foods consumed. Others are due to structural problems, that is, a problem that has occurred in the stomach or another part of the digestive system. Common problems are defined along with causes, symptoms, and treatments. Some stomach problems cannot be cured, so coping suggestions are discussed.

The second part of this book explores caring for your digestive system and improving the digestive process. It provides guidelines for when to see a doctor or when self-treatment is fine. You'll also learn about the role of diet, exercise, stress management, and other techniques for preventing or coping with tummy woes.

Common Stomach Problems

Just before study hall, Laura rubbed her stomach. "My stomach aches. I wonder if it's something I ate for lunch?" Just then she turned and headed down the hall.

"Hey, where are you going?" asked Tod.

"I've got to get to a bathroom," Laura shouted as she dashed away.

Most of us can relate to Laura's misery. Stomach problems often arise for both teens and adults. Sometimes the problem is handled easily and never reappears. For example, after Laura made it to the bathroom, she felt better. Her tummy gurgled a bit during the afternoon, but she did not have another bout of diarrhea that day. Since the unpleasant effects lasted only a short time, she forgot about her upset stomach by the next day. For others, though, their stomach problems may continue or even grow worse.

Causes

Like Laura, most people will never discover the cause of their infrequent stomach pains and upsets. Their problems are usually not serious, and most people recover in a day or two. But some digestive diseases may develop from birth or are caused by an infection. They may result from smoking or alcohol abuse. Both smoking and alcohol abuse—drinking too much alcohol too often—greatly increases the risk of developing digestive cancers.

Depending on the diagnosis, treatment options for stomach problems can vary. They can include prescription and nonprescription medicines, surgery, screening tests, waiting to see if the problem goes away, diet changes, exercise, chemotherapy, or home remedies.

Some digestive upsets can be avoided in the first place. The key to prevention is a healthy lifestyle. This includes eating well-balanced meals and snacks, rest and relaxation, and exercising regularly.

Who Develops a Digestive Disease?

The chances of developing a digestive disease increase with age. There are exceptions, however. For example, gastroenteritis generally hits infants and children more often than adults. Gastroenteritis is an infection or irritation of the stomach and intestines.

Females are more likely than males to report a digestive problem. Experts are unsure if this means it is a fact. That's because females tend to visit doctors more often than males, so they may tell their doctors more often about stomach problems.

Diagnosing Digestive Diseases

"We've got to find a bathroom. Now!"
"What's with you, Jared? I've stopped for you twice already, and it's only been an hour since the last

time." After Enrique drove to a nearby gas station, Jared hopped out of the car.

When he came back, Enrique asked, "How long has this been going on?"

"It's been a few weeks. Sometimes it isn't so bad, but other times I'll have diarrhea six or eight times a day. My stomach is upset a lot too, and it sometimes hurts."

Enrique shook his head. "You better get to a doctor. Something could be wrong."

Jared needs to see a doctor to get a diagnosis of his problem. Because most digestive diseases are complex, people may undergo extensive and expensive diagnostic tests. To reach a diagnosis, a doctor will require a thorough, accurate medical history and physical examination. Often laboratory tests are conducted These can include blood tests, an upper or lower gastrointestinal (GI) series of tests, an ultrasound, and endoscopic examinations of the stomach, esophagus, and other GI organs.

An endoscope is a small, flexible tube with a light and a lens on the end. For an upper GI examination, the endoscope is inserted into the patient's nose and is then moved down into the stomach. A doctor can look into the esophagus and stomach and, if needed, can take tissue from these organs for testing. Or using the endoscope, the doctor may take color photographs of these organs. For a lower GI examination, a sigmoidoscope, another type of tube, is inserted through the rectum and moved up into the colon and small intestine.

For complicated cases, a doctor may order sophisticated tests such as a computerized axial tomography, also called a CAT scan, or an MRI. A CAT scan is an X ray that produces three-dimensional pictures of the body. MRI, which stands for "magnetic resonance imaging," is a test that takes pictures of the soft tissues in the body. These pictures are clearer than X rays.

Choosing the Right Doctor

> Jared answered the ringing telephone. "Hi, this is Jared."
>
> "This is Dr. Miller. After running some blood tests and doing your physical exam, I recommend that you see a gastroenterologist."
>
> Jared interrupted. "What's wrong with me?"
>
> "I think you may have a digestive disease. As you know, I'm a primary care doctor. But I think the best doctor for you now is a gastroenterologist, a medical doctor with specialized training in the digestive system. These doctors are best equipped to answer your questions, run specialized tests, make a diagnosis, and prescribe the best treatment for you. I know some excellent GI doctors, Jared, so let's get you set up with one."

A primary care doctor can handle most treatment for basically healthy people. But a primary care doctor will sometimes refer people who may have a complex, chronic, or ongoing digestive problem to an gastroenterologist.

At this point Jared still does not know what digestive problem he may have. Depending on the results of various tests, he may have a digestive disease that will need treatment or other care. He may need to make some lifestyle and diet changes.

However, for most people their digestive problems are not long lasting or serious. You can learn to identify minor tummy woes, then manage them. Or better yet, you can learn to head them off before they rear up. If you have a digestive disease, learning to cope will help make you a stronger and healthier person.

"Ready for your driver's license test tomorrow?" *said Hannah as she unwrapped her sandwich.*

Cao played with her yogurt. "I don't think I'm going to take it. Something's wrong with my stomach. It's been hurting all day."

Hannah laughed. "You get so hyper about stuff! Relax, Cao. So what if you don't pass the driver's test tomorrow? You can always take it again."

Are you like Cao and get a stomach ache when you worry over something important? Does your tummy feel queasy when you're faced with a scary situation? Have you ever embarrassed yourself by passing gas? Maybe you've noticed that when you are really upset, your breath stinks.

Take Hannah's advice: Relax. Like most of us, you've probably had some minor tummy upsets. Most soon blow over. However, an upset stomach, bloating and feeling gassy, vomiting, or nausea can be nasty. Upset stomachs caused by too much food may respond to over-the-counter (OTC) medications. In other cases, seeing your doctor may be your best option.

Gas

Everyone has gas. Some people think they have too much gas when they really have normal amounts. Most people produce one to three pints of gas each day. We get rid of it by burping or passing it through the rectum.

> *"My stomach hurts," moaned Samaki.*
> *"My nose hurts," said Hunter, "from smelling you. What have you been eating?"*

Gas in the digestive system comes from two sources:

☞Swallowed air. We all swallow air when eating and drinking.

☞The normal breakdown of some foods by harmless bacteria naturally present in the large intestine, or colon. Sometimes the body can't digest and absorb certain carbohydrates—such as sugars, starches, and fiber—in the small intestine due to a shortage or absence of specific enzymes. When passed into the large intestine, bacteria that live there break down carbohydrates. In turn, various gases form such as hydrogen, carbon dioxide, nitrogen, oxygen, methane, and sulfur, which exit through the rectum. Any unpleasant odor comes from sulfur gas.

Most foods that contain carbohydrates can cause gas, but fats and proteins cause little gas. Also, foods that produce gas in one person may not cause gas in another. Here are some common gas culprits.

Gas-Producing Foods

Sugars that produce gas include raffinose, lactose, fructose, and sorbitol. Large amounts of raffinose are found in dried beans. Smaller amounts are found in cabbage, brussel sprouts, broccoli, cauliflower, asparagus, other vegetables, and whole grains. Lactose is the natural sugar in milk. It is also found in various milk products, such as cheese and ice cream, and in many processed foods, including bread, cereal, and salad dressings. Fructose occurs naturally in onions, artichokes, pears, and wheat and also is used as a sweetener in some soft drinks and fruit drinks. Sorbitol occurs naturally in fruits such as apples, pears, peaches, and prunes. It also is used as an artificial sweetener in many dietetic foods and sugarfree candies and gums.

Starches: Rice is the only starch that doesn't produce gas. Other starches, such as those in potatoes, corn, pasta, and wheat, produce gas.

Soluble fiber, which produces gas, dissolves in water, taking on a soft, gel-like texture in the intestines. It is found in oat bran, beans, peas, and most fruits. Soluble fiber is broken down in the colon. In contrast, insoluble fiber passes virtually unchanged through the intestines and produces little gas. Insoluble fiber is found in wheat bran and some vegetables.

More Than Gas

You probably remember the children's rhyme about beans: "Beans, beans, the magical fruit. The more you eat, the more you toot."

It is true that beans can cause gas—but only in some people, not all. Actually, having gas can mean that someone is experiencing all or some of these symptoms: belching, flatulence, stomach pain, and stomach bloating. Occasional bouts of any of these symptoms are normal. Chronic symptoms caused by too much gas or by a serious disease are rare. However, if gassiness is ongoing or if you notice a sharp increase in gassiness, see your doctor.

After dinner, Larry sometimes belches. "Just means I ate a good meal," he says. An occasional belch during or after meals is normal and releases gas when the stomach is full of food. However, many people who burp too much may be swallowing too much air and releasing it before the air enters the stomach. Sometimes people who burp a lot may have a digestive disorder such as an ulcer or reflux.

Cedric has another common complaint: "I pass gas. Too much, say my friends." Flatulence is the passage of too much gas through the rectum. What's too much? Probably not what you would imagine; most people pass gas fourteen to twenty-three times a day. Although rare, too much gas can result from severe carbohydrate malabsorption (inability to absorb carbohydrates in the intestines) or overactive bacteria in the colon.

Lori says, "I get bloated sometimes, and my stomach feels swollen." Many people believe that too much gas causes stomach bloating. However, people who complain of bloating from gas often have normal amounts. Instead these people may be sensitive, or unusually aware of, gas in their digestive system. Bloating can occur after eating a lot of fatty foods. This delays stomach emptying and causes bloating and discomfort but not necessarily too much gas.

Battling Gas

If you are troubled by too much gas, cut back on high-fat foods. By eating less pizza, hamburgers, fries, and other fatty foods, you reduce bloating and discomfort by helping the stomach empty faster, which moves gases into the small intestine sooner. And avoid carbonated beverages; they cause gas.

Over-the-counter medicines can sometimes provide gas relief. These include:

- Simethicone—a foaming agent that joins gas bubbles in the stomach so that gas is more easily passed on. It has no effect on intestinal gas.

- Activated charcoal—this may provide relief from gas in the colon. Take just before eating and soon after a meal.

- Digestive enzymes—lactase enzymes or sugar-digesting enzymes may allow people to eat foods that normally cause gas. These enzymes come in liquid, tablet, and caplet form.

For people who burp too much, reducing swallowed air may help. Air swallowing is a common cause of gas in the stomach. To reduce air swallowing, avoid chewing gum and sucking on hard candy, and eat at a slow pace. And don't smoke.

Brad says, "I swallow air to make myself belch. Doesn't this help?" No, it doesn't. It only adds to the amount of air in the stomach and doesn't stop you from burping.

Dragon Breath

Stacy, the tenth-grade clown, was telling a great joke before the first-period bell. She noticed several people backing away from her. Later she asked her best friend, Carolyn, "What's the problem? Do I have bad breath?"

Carolyn frowned. "I hate to be the one to tell you this, but since you asked, yes, sometimes your breath smells, especially in the morning."

Stacy's face turned red. "I didn't know I had dragon breath!"

Bad breath, or halitosis, usually comes from the millions of bacteria that live in your mouth. As these bacteria break down the food you've eaten, they give off bad-smelling gases such as hydrogen sulfide, which smells like rotten eggs. Your saliva usually washes away food bits and any smell.

Stacy's halitosis, though, is caused by hunger odor. Her bad breath develops while she sleeps, when juices from her pancreas go into her stomach. If Stacy stopped skipping breakfast in the morning, her bad breath would go away, since this foul odor disappears after eating.

Another dragon breath culprit is eating strong foods, such as onions, garlic, or horseradish. These foods can revisit by causing bad breath several hours later, after they are absorbed into the bloodstream and the odors are carried to your lungs.

Ever get so stressed that your breath smells terrible? Under heavy stress your saliva stops working. Your mouth dries out, and the bacteria stay in your mouth.

Another cause of bad breath can result from gum disease, especially if your gums bleed.

To deal with bad breath, clean and floss your teeth regularly. Drink lots of water throughout the day to keep your saliva going and to wash away odor-causing bacteria. And be sure to eat in the morning and every three to four hours after that so your empty tummy doesn't send up hunger odors.

Plugged Up!

Ever have a bad week when things seem to be going wrong, you're not eating well, and you're not having regular bowel movements? You may be temporarily constipated. Constipation is the passage of small amounts of hard, dry bowel movements, usually fewer than three times a week. People who are constipated find it difficult and painful to have a bowel movement. They also may feel bloated, uncomfortable, and sluggish.

Stool Stories

Many people think that they are constipated when they aren't. "If I don't go every day, I know something's wrong," declares Carrie. Not true. There is no right number of daily or weekly bowel movements. One person may go two or three times a day, and someone else might go every other day. And some people naturally have firmer stools than others. Most of us get constipated at one time or another. Generally most cases of constipation are temporary and not serious. Your body will correct itself within a short time.

21

However, many people waste money on OTC laxatives, which are medicines used to relieve constipation. In fact, Americans spend $725 million each year on laxatives. But instead of flushing your money away, you can head off or cope with many common causes of constipation.

Keeping Regular

Constipation, although unpleasant, rarely indicates a serious health problem. For most people it's a temporary nuisance. You can take charge to make sure that your bouts of constipation are infrequent or nonexistent. Here are some causes of constipation and what to do if it strikes you:

⮡Poor diet: What do you get if you eat a diet high in animal fats (meats, dairy products, and eggs) and sugar (rich desserts and other sweets) but low in fiber? You could get constipation. Poor diet is the number one cause of constipation among American teens and adults. To avoid potential problems, eat plenty of fiber-rich foods, such as vegetables, fruits, beans, and whole grains.

⮡ Lack of fluids: Surprisingly, if you don't drink enough water every day, you could trigger constipation. Water adds fluid to the colon and bulk to stools, making bowel movements softer and easier to pass. Drink about eight 8-ounce glasses each day. Alcohol and liquids that contain caffeine—such as coffee, soft drinks, and carbonated beverages—tend to dry out your system and contribute to constipation.

⮫ Lack of exercise: Regular exercise helps keep your digestive system working smoothly. Researchers aren't sure why lack of exercise leads to constipation.

⮫ Medications: Some OTC and prescription medications can bring on constipation. These include narcotics, antacids that contain aluminum, antispasmodics, antidepressants, iron supplements, diuretics, and anticonvulsants for epilepsy. If this is a problem for you, talk to your doctor.

⮫ Laxative abuse: Regular use of laxatives is unnecessary and can be habit-forming. The colon begins to rely on laxatives to bring on bowel movements and, over time, will fail to work properly. Avoid laxatives unless your doctor prescribes them.

⮫ Poor bowel habits: Got to go, but too busy? Don't abuse your body by ignoring its signals. If you continue to ignore the urge to have a bowel movement, eventually you may stop feeling the urge, leading to chronic constipation.

⮫ Travel: Ever stayed overnight in a strange place and couldn't have a bowel movement when you needed to? People often become temporarily constipated when traveling or in unfamiliar surroundings. If this happens, don't worry. Your system will soon return to normal.

⮫ Specific diseases: Some diseases can cause constipation, including neurological (nerve) disorders, metabolic and endocrine disorders, and diseases that affect the body tissues. Talk to your doctor if this problem affects you.

When You Have to Go. . .

What's the opposite of constipation and has hit most of us at one time or another? Diarrhea, which is frequent, watery discharge from the bowels. It seldom lasts longer than a few days and is often caused by food poisoning, nervous shock, stress, or a variety of illnesses such as the flu. Eating artificial fats also can set off diarrhea and stomach cramping because these substances aren't absorbed by the body. Traveler's diarrhea can attack if you are away from home and eating unfamiliar foods, foods not thoroughly cooked, or foods that haven't been cleaned properly, or drinking unclean water.

Foodborne or waterborne protozoa and bacteria may be the culprits in many cases of diarrhea. Protozoa are small one-celled organisms. The protozoan *Giardia lamblia* heads the list of waterborne agents that cause diarrhea. Giardiasis results in loose and smelly stools, cramps, and bad-tasting burps along with a loss of energy, appetite, and weight. Treatment usually involves antibiotics. Another protozoan, *Cryptosporidium*, strikes with cramps, nausea, gas, and diarrhea; this lasts about a week.

Escherichia coli, a common bacterium that lives in your stomach, has a few types that can cause diarrhea. For example, *E coli*, which is typically swallowed in water, produces headache, nausea, and foul-smelling diarrhea soon after ingestion. Luckily, in most cases you're back to health in one to three days. However, illness from *E coli* bacteria can be more severe. In recent years *E coli* has been linked to several deaths in the United States. In those cases, illness resulted from ingesting *E coli* from under-cooked hamburger meat.

Salmonella is another type of bacteria that strikes about 2.5 million people each year in the United States. Usually the person eats food contaminated with the bacteria, especially dairy products, poultry, meat, and eggs. The unpleasant results—headache, fever, nausea, cramps, and diarrhea—typically disappear within a few days, although the health consequences can be more severe.

When It Strikes

All people with diarrhea, whatever its cause, experience one thing in common: the loss of a lot of fluid along with potassium and sodium. So if diarrhea strikes, the most important treatment is to drink plenty of liquids. Your best choices are clear liquids, such as water and soup broth, and clear fruit juices. As the diarrhea subsides and your appetite perks up, opt for soft, bland, low-fat cooked foods, including cereals, baked or mashed potatoes, soft-boiled eggs, and so on. Avoid alcohol, caffeine, spices, fruits, hard cheeses, and other fat-laden products.

You usually don't need to take over-the-counter medications for diarrhea, since most cases last a short time. Pepto-Bismol can help relieve some discomfort, but often it turns stools black. Immodium or Lomotil are over-the-counter drugs that reduce cramps and the frequency and volume of stools. Don't use these medications beyond what is recommended on the product label. If you experience severe diarrhea, bloody stools, high fever, or continuous vomiting, see your doctor. Your doctor may prescribe an antispasmodic medication that will help relax your colon.

Heading It Off

Keys to diarrhea prevention involve proper food handling and hygiene. Promptly refrigerate leftover food to slow the growth of potentially harmful bacteria. Always wash your hands with soap and water after you use the bathroom and before preparing food. Don't share personal items such as cups and eating utensils. Keep anyone who is ill out of the kitchen. Use plenty of hot, soapy water to wash dishes, then rinse them well in fresh water.

If you are unsure of the risks of food- or waterborne bacteria and protozoa, pay attention to your foods and beverages. Uncooked foods are risky, particularly raw vegetables and raw or undercooked meats and seafood. Other suspect items include ice made from tap water, unpasteurized milk and other dairy products, and unpeeled fruits. Stick to bottled beverages, herbal teas, or water that has been boiled sufficiently or treated with iodine or chlorine.

Irritable Bowel Syndrome

By the time Cao got to her driver's test, she didn't feel good. "When I feel stressed, I get stomach cramps and diarrhea or periods of constipation," she says. Cao has irritable bowel syndrome (IBS). IBS is also called spastic colon or colitis. Because IBS is caused by a problem in how the intestines work, it is considered a digestive disorder, not a disease.

Although IBS is not life-threatening, it can affect the quality of life for some people. Cao sometimes avoids doing things with her friends. "I worry where the bathrooms are when I go out with my friends. It's a nuisance for everyone when I have to take a lot of bathroom breaks to deal with my IBS."

What It Is

The National Institutes of Health estimate that five million Americans have IBS. This common disorder can cause intermittent symptoms such as cramps, stomach pain, gassiness, bloating, excess mucus in the stools, and changes in bowel habits. Some people with IBS are constipated, whereas others experience diarrhea. Some people experience both or alternate between the two conditions. Sometimes people with IBS have an urge to move their bowels but cannot.

Researchers are not sure what causes IBS. It appears that nerves that control the muscles in the digestive tract become too active, so that people with IBS have a colon that is more sensitive and reactive than usual. In other words, their colon responds more strongly to stimuli that don't bother most people. For example, most people report that their IBS kicks in following a meal or when they are under stress. Caffeine, chocolate, milk products, and large amounts of alcohol are the worst offenders.

No specific medical test exists to diagnose IBS. Instead doctors make their diagnosis of IBS after ruling out more serious diseases. They do this by taking a medical history, completing a physical examination, and running various laboratory tests. You also may be examined by your doctor with a sigmoidoscope.

During this exam you lay on your side. The doctor inserts a sigmoidoscope—a thin, flexible fiber-optic tube—into your rectum and slowly eases it up into the colon. The doctor can see your colon through the sigmoidoscope. During this examination the doctor is looking for any signs of inflammation or sores along your colon. However, people with IBS typically show no sign of physical problems with their colon.

If nothing abnormal is found after all medical tests are run, IBS is probably the culprit. Unfortunately no cure for IBS exists at the present time. Although IBS causes a lot of discomfort and distress, it does not cause permanent harm to the stomach or intestines. It also does not lead to a more serious disease, such as cancer, or to inflammatory bowel diseases, such as Crohn's disease or ulcerative colitis.

Crohn's disease causes severe irritation in the digestive tract. As the mucous lining of the digestive tract becomes inflamed, absorption of digested food is seriously hampered. This chronic disease requires medical attention. Ulcerative colitis is a serious disease that causes ulcers and irritation in the inner lining of the colon and rectum. Most people with IBS can control their symptoms through diet, lifestyle changes, stress management, and sometimes with prescription medications.

Ulcerative colitis, sometimes called colitis, is inflammation of the colon. Symptoms include constant diarrhea, often with blood and mucous; stomach pain; and sometimes fever. Medical treatment is required to treat this chronic disease.

What You Can Do

There is no standard way to treat IBS. That's because of two reasons: Health experts are not sure of its causes, and symptoms vary considerably among people with IBS. Moderate, regular exercise can help provide relief from IBS for some people. Exercise keeps your digestive system running smoothly, which in turn keeps IBS from flaring up. Maintaining regular bowel habits is another technique that can help keep IBS at bay.

One known cause of IBS is tobacco. That's because nicotine is an irritant to the digestive tract and triggers IBS symptoms. The air swallowed during smoking can contribute to excess gas. So if you smoke and have IBS, stop smoking.

Diet often plays an important role in coping with IBS. For example, researchers have found that the strength of the IBS response is often related to the number of calories in a meal, especially the amount of fat consumed. Fat, whether from animal or vegetable, strongly stimulates contractions in the colon after a meal. In turn, this can cause an IBS reaction. Many foods contain fats, especially meats, poultry skin, whole milk and other high-fat dairy foods, vegetable oil, shortening, and avocados. However, some people find that cultured dairy products do not trigger their IBS. Cultured dairy foods include buttermilk, sour cream, and yogurt.

Some people report that avoiding spicy foods; artificial fats; artificial sweeteners such as sorbitol, mannitol, and xylitol; fructose; caffeine-laced foods and beverages; and carbonated beverages helps keep their IBS under control. Lactose (the sugar in milk products) and alcohol can also trigger IBS in many people.

Eating plenty of dietary fiber tends to lessen IBS symptoms for some people. "By eating whole grain breads and cereals, and plenty of beans, fruits, and vegetables, I usually can keep my IBS from popping up," reports Leslie. Whenever you add more fiber to your diet, be sure to drink plenty of water—at least six to eight glasses a day. Also, Leslie now eats smaller meals five or six times a day. She discovered that "large meals cause cramping and diarrhea for me."

Here are a few other food tips that help with IBS:

- Eat at regular times and every three to four hours.
- Don't overeat.
- Try to avoid foods that are overly spicy or cold foods that can cause excess gas.

Stress also stimulates spasms in the colon for people with IBS, a process that is not completely understood. However, since the colon is controlled partly by the nervous system, people have found that stress reduction methods and relaxation techniques can help relieve the symptoms of IBS. This does not mean that IBS is the result of a personality disorder. Instead, IBS is partly a disorder of the colon and how well it works. Stress, therefore, does not cause IBS, but it can trigger symptoms.

Medical Treatment

Sheryl says, "After my doctor told me that I had irritable

bowel syndrome, he said I needed to increase my daily fiber by taking over-the-counter fiber supplements. These supplements come in pill, caplet, or powder form. He also offered to prescribe an antidepressant medication for me, but I thought I'd try the other things first to see how well they work." Fiber supplements, typically derived from psyllium seed, include Citrucel or Metamucil. If you take fiber supplements, drink plenty of water. Without enough water, the extra fiber can make stools hard and difficult to pass.

Some doctors prescribe low-dose antidepressants or tranquilizers to help relax the colon as a way to treat IBS. People with IBS may find that taking antispasmodic medications on an as-needed basis are helpful. These are prescription drugs that relax the colon. Jenny, for example, says, "I take my antispasmodic before I eat rather than after my symptoms kick in. This works pretty well in preventing an IBS attack." Sometimes doctors may prescribe over-the-counter fiber supplements or occasional laxatives for people with IBS who have bouts of constipation.

However, drug treatment for IBS is not the final answer. That's because any medication may produce unwanted side effects. For example, some people may become dependent on tranquilizers or laxatives, needing more and more until their colon cannot function normally. Tranquilizers and antidepressants can cause drowsiness, and antispasmodics cause constipation. Since IBS is a chronic condition of yet unknown causes, medication treatment is generally best saved for times of severe symptoms.

Taming Motion Sickness

"I was excited to go walleye fishing on Lake Superior," recalled Bryan. *"But once our small boat left the shore, I started feeling queasy. I remember one of my friends saying I looked pale. As the boat sped over the choppy waters, I got so dizzy that I lay down. I was fighting not to vomit. By this time my face had turned a greenish color.*

"I begged to go back to land. Once I got off the boat, I started feeling better, but it took about twenty or thirty minutes before I felt well enough to get up and walk around."

What Bryan experienced is called motion sickness. This condition can affect anyone at any age. Usually paleness, yawning, and restlessness precede the nausea, vomiting, and dizziness of full-blown motion sickness. The main culprit in this condition is excess stimulation in the inner ear's fluid-filled cavities, which are responsible for maintaining the body's balance. As in Bryan's case, motion sickness can be triggered by unusual motion, poor ventilation, anxiety or other emotional upset, or visual stimuli. Although unpleasant, motion sickness is not life-threatening, nor does it trigger other health conditions.

Heading It Off

It is easier to prevent motion sickness than to treat it once it has begun. Sometimes you may not know that you're prone to motion sickness until you experience it. However, if you know this can be a problem for you, try these tips:

- Don't read while in motion (on a car, boat, airplane, etc.).

- Keep your line of vision straight ahead as much as possible.

- Avoid excess food before and during a long trip.

- Avoid all food and beverages on any short trips.

- When you travel stay where motion is least felt, such as the front seat of a car, near the wings of an airplane, or amidship, preferably on deck.

- Don't smoke and try not to breathe unusual odors, particularly from foods or tobacco smoke.

Once It Strikes

Stopping, or removing the motion sickness trigger, is usually enough to stop the unpleasant symptoms. But if you have to travel, for example, and you get motion sickness, you can try OTC medications to deal with the unpleasant symptoms. There are four active ingredients that work for motion sickness:

- cyclizine (Maurezine and others)

- dimenhydrinate (Dramamine and others)

- diphenhydramine (Benadryl and others)

- meclizine (Bonine and others)

All four of these medications have something in common—they are antihistamines. Their main unwanted side effect is drowsiness. Taking alcohol, tranquilizers, or sedatives along with any of these four may increase drowsiness. If you have to take large doses, or amounts, of these medications for motion sickness, you also may get dry mouth and blurred vision. These medications can take thirty to sixty minutes to take effect. That's why it is best to take them before you begin to travel and then continue the dosage, if needed, during traveling.

Heartburn and Beyond

"Over here!" Angie waved at Marita across the crowded restaurant.

Everyone moved closer to make room for Marita as she slid into the circular booth. "We already ordered pizza," said Angie. "The special sounded good, so we went with that—sausage, pepperoni, onion, roasted garlic, green pepper, and hot pepper."

The four juniors ate their Guistio's Special pizza, along with soft drinks and garlic bread. Soon, though, Angie noticed Marita frantically digging through her purse. "What's wrong?" Angie asked her friend.

"Whenever I eat spicy foods like this, I get a burning pain in my chest, but these help." Marita popped two tablets into her mouth and chewed.

Alejandro looked at his alarm clock. 3 AM. Again. It was the third time this week that he had woken in the middle of the night with a bad acid taste in his mouth. This time it felt as if he had some sour-tasting food in his mouth.

Once inside the bathroom, he spit out the stuff, then drank some water. He headed back to his room. With a sigh he reached for the bottle of antacid stowed under his bed. He'd have to remember to buy more the next day.

Heartburn and GERD

Although Alejandro and Marita have different symptoms, both are suffering from heartburn. The name of this particular stomach disorder is a misnomer: Heartburn has nothing to do with the heart. Instead it's caused by stomach acid flowing back into the esophagus. Ongoing heartburn may be a symptom of a disease called gastroesophageal reflux disease (GERD). "Gastroesophageal" refers to the stomach and esophagus. "Reflux" means "to flow back or return." So gastroesophageal reflux is the return of the stomach's contents back up into the esophagus.

In the course of normal digestion, the lower esophageal sphincter (LES) muscle does its job every time you eat or drink beverages. This muscle connects the esophagus with the stomach. When food or liquids are swallowed, the LES opens. This allows food or liquid to pass into the stomach. Then it closes, preventing food and acidic stomach juices from flowing back up the esophagus.

GERD occurs when the LES is weak or does not tighten correctly. This allows the stomach's contents to move up into the esophagus. Over time, inflammation of the esophageal lining can result, and sores may form there. Due to inflammation, the esophagus becomes more sensitive to acid, which can lead to more painful heartburn.

Chronic heartburn is the most common symptom of GERD. Other symptoms include regurgitation of gastric acid or sour contents into the mouth, difficult or painful swallowing, chest pain, and a sore throat. "I've noticed that my heartburn usually gets worse after eating," says Larry. "Also, it appears if I bend over or lie down." Beth's

36

heartburn problems are different. "I burp a lot. It's embarrassing at times, but usually I can laugh it off."

GERD, however, is not a laughing matter. Left untreated, it can cause serious problems, including the following:

- ➥ Stomach acid that reaches the mouth can dissolve tooth enamel.

- ➥ Esophagitis, or inflammation of the esophagus lining, can occur from too much stomach acid in the esophagus. Esophagitis may cause esophageal bleeding or ulcers.

- ➥ The esophagus can become scarred, which results in narrowing of the tube. If this happens, a person could have difficulty swallowing food or liquids.

- ➥ Bleeding in the stomach. Symptoms include vomiting blood or stool turning black, which indicates that blood is passing through the digestive system.

- ➥ Choking, shortness of breath, coughing, and hoarseness due to acid refluxed into the windpipe.

- ➥ Lung damage if acid is refluxed into the windpipe and into the lungs.

- ➥ Barrett's esophagus, a precancerous change in the esophagus lining. Over time, Barrett's sometimes turns into esophageal cancer.

Although GERD can limit daily activities for some people, it is rarely life-threatening. There is no cure for GERD.

Have You Experienced Heartburn?

Marita experiences heartburn occasionally. If she eats spicy foods, within a hour or less, she feels heartburn. "It's like a burning chest pain. The pain begins behind my breastbone and rises up to my neck and throat. This can last for several hours after I eat."

Alejandro has never had chest pain. Instead, he says, "My heartburn feels like bits of sour food coming back into my mouth. I have an acid or bitter taste in my mouth. Also, I wake up with a sore throat."

The burning, pressure, or pain of heartburn can last as long as a few hours. It is often worse after eating. Sometimes the acid backing into the mouth does not occur until the person lies down. In fact, lying down or bending over can cause heartburn in some people.

Heartburn pain can be mistaken for a heart attack. Joe's dad was rushed to the hospital emergency room when he began complaining of severe chest pains. Everyone thought he was having a heart attack. Instead he developed bad heartburn after eating a big meal of fried chicken and fries.

Like Alejandro, some people wake up at night with heartburn. This often is the result of filling the stomach with food or liquid before lying down. Even when you're asleep, reflux can occur.

Who Gets Heartburn or GERD?

Like Marita, many people get occasional heartburn. According to the National Institute of Diabetes and Digestive and Kidney Diseases in Bethesda, Maryland, more than 60 million Americans experience heartburn at least once a month. Of those, about 25 million have heartburn every day. This chronic heartburn is called GERD. At least a quarter or more of pregnant women get daily heartburn. GERD can affect anyone, at any age, and of ethnic group, sex, or socioeconomic class. Experts are not yet sure if it's hereditary (passed down in families).

Once thought to be a disease that only affected adults, doctors now know that babies, children, and teens can have GERD. Infants and children with GERD may not show typical adult GERD symptoms. Instead they may regularly vomit, cough, or have respiratory problems. Or they may eat poorly and lose weight. Other signs of heartburn in babies and children include frequent spitting up or vomiting, poor weight gain, weight loss, frequent red or sore throat, swallowing problems, bad breath, choking, and gagging.

Causes of GERD

Hiatal Hernia

Experts do not know exactly what causes all cases of heartburn or GERD. Some doctors think a hiatal hernia is the culprit. A hiatal hernia is a small opening in the diaphragm that allows the upper part of the stomach to move up into the chest. The diaphragm is the muscle that separates the stomach from the chest. The hernia causes heartburn by allowing stomach acid to flow back up through the opening.

A hiatal hernia also weakens the lower esophageal sphincter muscle, which leads to reflux. A hiatal hernia causes acid and other stomach contents to be retained above its opening. These substances can move up into the esophagus.

Some people can develop a hiatal hernia from coughing, vomiting, straining, or sudden physical exertion. "I was surprised when my doctor told me that I'd caused a hiatal hernia from my power weight lifting," says King. These activities can cause increased pressure in the abdomen, leading to a hiatal hernia.

Many people over the age of fifty have a small hiatal hernia. However, anyone at any age can develop one. Most hiatal hernias do not cause any problems and never require treatment.

Other Factors

There are three other known causes of GERD. One is cigarette smoking. Cigarette smoking is known to relax the diaphragm. The other two factors that can cause GERD are obesity and pregnancy. Many pregnant women experience heartburn because their internal organs are squeezed for space due to the growing baby. Most such cases of heartburn disappear after birth.

Some doctors think that other factors can lead to heartburn and GERD. Certain beverages and foods, such as chocolate, mints, greasy foods, coffee, and alcohol, may weaken the lower esophageal sphincter muscle, leading to heartburn. Over time this could result in GERD.

Seventeen-year-old Linda says, "I was eight years old and having digestive problems—now I know I was refluxing. Back then, my puzzled doctor had me see a psychologist who concluded that I was stressed out and that's what was causing my problems." Stress does not cause GERD.

Treating Heartburn: OTC Medications

"I've found that taking antacids after eating spicy foods relieves my heartburn," Marita says. "But sometimes I only feel partial relief. Should I take something else?"

For infrequent heartburn such as Marita's, taking an occasional antacid when needed is fine. Antacids are OTC medicines that neutralize acid in the esophagus and stomach and help stop heartburn.

Since Marita is getting only partial relief, she may want to try an antacid combined with a foaming agent, such as alginic acid. These compounds form a foam barrier on top of the stomach, which can help prevent acid reflux from occurring.

But you need to be careful. Using antacids for more than three weeks or more than two or three times a week regularly is not a good idea. That's because over time, these medicines can cause unwanted effects. These can include diarrhea; excessive buildup of magnesium in the body, which is serious for people with kidney disease; and altered calcium metabolism, or a change in the way your body breaks down and uses calcium. If you're using antacids this frequently, you need to talk to your doctor.

Other OTC medications may help with infrequent heartburn. These medications, called H2 blockers, are sold under the brand names Tagamet HB, Zantac 75, Pepcid AC, and Axid AR. "I've seen TV ads in which different brands claim that they're better or work faster than others. Is any of this true?" asks Julie. All OTC H2 blockers work the same way—by inhibiting the secretion of acid in the stomach. Studies also show that they are virtually identical

41

in how fast they work. So ignore the television and radio advertisements that promote how much faster one H2 blocker is compared to another.

H2 blockers can bring relief from heartburn for up to eight hours. These medicines take thirty to forty minutes to work, which means you need to take them about a half-hour before eating. "If I forget to take my meds before I eat spicy food, then right after I eat, I take an antacid. This works okay," Aaron says. If you have already eaten and are experiencing heartburn, an H2 blocker will not help.

Infrequent heartburn—once a month—is usually no cause for concern. But if you're stockpiling heartburn pills, that's a good indication that you need medical help. Anyone who takes OTC H2 blockers more than two or three times a week needs to see a doctor for medical evaluation. Such constant heartburn or reflux can indicate a more serious problem, such as GERD, which can lead to serious complications if left untreated.

Treating GERD: Lifestyle Changes

After Dr. Smythe, the gastroenterologist, got back Alejandro's test results, she met with him. (A gastroenterologist is a physician who specializes in the treatment of the stomach and digestive system.) "Alejandro, you have GERD," she told him. "In a nutshell, that's chronic heartburn, which is what wakes you up at night. Antacids are okay as a first line of treatment, but they're not effective or safe for long-term treatment."

"So should I stop taking them?" Alejandro asked.

"Yes. Let's talk about some dietary and lifestyle

changes. They may help decrease your reflux and reduce the damage to the lining of your esophagus from refluxed materials. I also have this written up, but we'll go over it now in case you have questions."

Diet Culprits

Dr. Smythe continued. "Let's tackle diet first. Avoid chocolate, peppermint, fatty foods, coffee, and alcoholic beverages. They can weaken the sphincter muscle. Also avoid foods and beverages that can irritate your damaged esophageal lining—that means citrus fruits, tomato products, and pepper."

As he listened, Alejandro looked sadder and sadder. "I don't drink coffee or alcohol, but how can I live without chocolate?"

Dr. Smythe smiled. "Not everyone has a problem with all of these foods. You may be able to eat a small amount of chocolate once in while."

Dr. Smythe recommended that Alejandro decrease the size of his portions and spread out his meals. So instead of eating three big meals each day, Alejandro will eat five or six smaller meals or snacks. By eating less, the sphincter muscle can hold food in the stomach more easily.

Dairy foods such as milk, cheese, and ice cream can actually trigger heartburn in some people. The calcium in dairy products stimulates acid production. Also, many dairy foods are high in fat. However, not everyone reacts to certain foods the same way. "I can eat a three-scoop ice cream cone without heartburn," says Scott. " But I have to pull my fork away from spaghetti or chili."

Lavia sighed. "I can eat a few fries, but that's my limit. I can't eat even half an order of fries, or I'll be miserable. It'll feel like sharp cuts in my stomach."

Other Methods

Other simple changes also may bring relief. Stay away from tight-fitting clothes and belts that constrict the stomach. Avoid heavy lifting and straining.

Alejandro figured out something else to help his reflux. "I avoid lying down for three to four hours after eating. This gives my stomach time to digest food, and I don't go to bed with a full stomach. This has made a difference for me." Here's why this works: As your stomach empties, acid production slows down, which lessens the chance of refluxing.

Some people sleep with their head higher than their feet. Gravity helps to keep stomach juices from backing up. Alejandro explains: "First I elevated the head of my bed on six-inch blocks. It took me about a week to get used to sleeping with my head higher than my feet. Then I switched to a specially designed wedge-shaped pillow I found at a local home health care equipment-and-supply business."

If you smoke, stop! Smoking weakens the sphincter muscle and irritates the lining of the esophagus. Tobacco also may stimulate acid production. And drinking alcohol, no matter what kind, usually heightens reflux symptoms.

Another major factor is obesity, which can aggravate GERD. Losing weight can help with reflux because it reduces the pressure on the abdomen that leads to reflux. Many overweight people find relief when they shed pounds.

Heartburn or GERD: What to Avoid

Although not everyone reacts the same to these substances, all of them have been found to contribute to heartburn or GERD in some people:

- Alcoholic beverages

- Fried, greasy, or fatty foods

- Chocolate and cocoa

- Coffee, both regular and decaffeinated

- Mints, including peppermint and spearmint

- Citrus juices or fruits

- Tomato products including tomato sauce and ketchup

- Carbonated beverages

- Mustard

- Onions, raw or cooked

- Garlic, raw or cooked

- Vinegar, especially vinegar-laced sauces and dressings

- Spicy foods, including pizza, chili, salsa, and curry

- Aspirin and other pain relievers (Acetaminophen, which is the active ingredient in Tylenol, is okay.)

↝ Some asthma and heart medications. (Check with your doctor or pharmacist.)

Treating GERD: Prescription Medicines

Dr. Smythe explained to Alejandro that "GERD is a disease, so it usually can't be handled by lifestyle changes alone. That's why I'll have you try an H2 blocker prescription medication. It's the same as the OTC version, but at a higher dose."

"How will I know if it's working?"Alejandro asked.

"You should feel better within a couple of days. If you're still having symptoms after that, call me, and we'll try another medicine."

H2 blockers were the first prescription medicines used to treat GERD. H2 blockers interfere with histamine, one of three chemical messengers that signal stomach cells to churn out acid. In the late 1990s, more powerful medicines hit the market. These prescription drugs, called proton-pump inhibitors, are acid reducers.

Prilosec and Prevacid, two proton-pump inhibitors, prevent all three chemical messengers from producing acid. This almost completely shuts down stomach acid production. Another type of prescription drug used to treat GERD is promotility agents. These drugs, such as Propulsid, increase the rate at which the stomach empties, giving the acid less chance to reflux.

Ask your doctor when to expect results. Most of these drugs work quickly and should help within days. Other drugs may take longer before kicking in.

What If Symptoms Continue?

For over a year, eighteen-year-old Lydell has been taking prescription medicines to treat his GERD. "During the first year, they worked great," he says. "Then I started getting heartburn at night. So I started popping antacid tablets in addition to my prescription medicines. When I told my gastroenterologist, she upped my prescription dosage. That didn't help. I tried other medicines, but nothing helped."

Like Lydell, some people with chronic GERD may find that their prescription medicines no longer work or that such drugs never worked well in the first place. Trying a stronger dose, changing the time when the medicine is taken, or taking a different medicine sometimes helps. In Lydell's case, because medications were no longer helping, his gastroenterologist required a complete evaluation to determine what was going on. Doctors use a variety of tests and procedures to evaluate GERD.

An upper GI series may be performed. This test is a special X ray that shows the esophagus, stomach, and upper part of the small intestine. Some people undergo twenty-four-hour pH monitoring. This procedure measures the acid levels inside the esophagus over a twenty-four-hour period. This is done by placing a thin tube in the esophagus, which is connected to a small computer that records pH level changes. Endoscopy is another procedure commonly done in people who do not respond well to GERD medications.

"I had an endoscopy," said Lydell. "I couldn't eat or drink anything the night before. At the clinic the

gastroenterologist inserted a narrow, lighted tube through my nose, down my esophagus. I didn't feel anything because I was given a light anesthetic that made me relaxed and a little drowsy."

The tube had a camera at the end so that the doctor could see any inflammation or irritation on the lining of the esophagus. She also took a biopsy—a small sample of tissue—from Lydell's lower esophagus. The whole procedure took about twenty-five or thirty minutes. Lydell remembered, "After the endoscopy, I had a slight sore throat for a few days, but I felt fine otherwise."

Another Treatment Option: Surgery

Lydell admitted that when his doctor called a week later with test results, "I was scared. She said I had Barrett's esophagus and that I needed to think about having surgery."

Lydell's GERD had become much worse, causing Barrett's esophagus. In this disease the normal lining of the esophagus is damaged or destroyed as a result of chronic acid reflux. To replace the normal lining, the stomach lining grows into the esophagus. This is abnormal growth, which shows up in an endoscopic exam and in a biopsy. (A biopsy is the removal of living cells or tissue from the body for the purpose of diagnosis.)

Barrett's esophagus occurs in about 10 percent of people with GERD. Compared to females, males are more likely to develop this disease. It usually is discovered in people over the age of 55, but this disease can affect teens and young children. If left untreated, 5 to 10 percent of people with Barrett's esophagus will develop esophageal cancer. However, the risk of developing this cancer is low, since the odds of developing Barrett's are also low.

Because medications were no longer helping, laparoscopic surgery was Lydell's next step. This surgery is also an option for people with GERD who have not responded well to prescription medicines and lifestyle changes.

The night before his surgery, Lydell could not eat or drink anything. After checking into the hospital the next morning, he was given an anesthetic that would put him to sleep for the duration of the surgery. To start, the surgeon made five one-inch cuts into Lydell's abdomen. Through one of the cuts, he inserted a laparoscope, a small telescope, which allowed him to see clearly into Lydell's abdomen. He placed small surgical instruments through the other cuts. During the surgery, which usually lasts two to four hours, the doctor wrapped the very top of the stomach around Lydell's esophagus. This strengthens the existing sphincter valve.

Afterward, Lydell recalled, "I didn't remember anything about the surgery. I stayed in the hospital for three days, recovering. After that I stayed home for a week. I slept a lot and ate only liquids—clear soups, puddings, Jell-O, things like that. Then I returned to school. By this time I was eating regular solid foods. I can still remember how exciting it was to eat my first hamburger!

"During my follow-up visit, the surgeon explained
that he hadn't cut through any muscle, which is why
the pain wasn't as bad as I had imagined it would be.
He also told me that since I didn't get any stitches,
the scars would fade almost completely."

Even after successful surgery, Lydell is not cured of
Barrett's esophagus or GERD. He will need to be
screened by having an endoscopy every one to two years,
to make sure that his Barrett's does not get worse or
develop into cancer. "I still need to avoid spicy and fatty
foods, just like before. But it's a huge relief not to wake
up at night with heartburn."

St. Margaret Middle School Library
1716-A Churchville Road
Bel Air, Maryland 21015

Peptic Ulcers: The Good News

"What's wrong?" Jardine asked. "You keep clutching your middle."

Tenzin shrugged. "I don't know how to describe this. I feel sick to my stomach. And for weeks I've felt a gnawing pain just above my belly button."

Jardine pulled something from her pocket. "Try one. It's an antacid. They help when I get heartburn."

"No, thanks. I've tried antacids, but they don't help. Maybe it's something besides heartburn."

After Tenzin went through some medical tests and an examination, she found out that she had a peptic ulcer, commonly called an ulcer. Ulcers in the stomach are called gastric ulcers. When an ulcer forms where the stomach joins the small intestine, it's called a duodenal ulcer. Gastric and duodenal ulcers together are called peptic ulcers.

"Peptic ulcers are common," explained Tenzin's doctor. "One in every ten Americans develops one at some time. An ulcer is a sore, usually round, on the stomach lining. Think of your ulcer like a sunburn on your stomach. That sore or hole peels away your protective stomach lining. Then the fragile tissue underneath gets hit over and over with your stomach acid, which keeps it irritated, causing you pain."

Ulcer Symptoms

Like Tenzin and Jardine, some people confuse heartburn and gastroesophageal reflux disease (GERD) symptoms with ulcer symptoms. But the two differ. Ulcer symptoms include:

↪ A gnawing pain or discomfort in the upper abdomen, between the bottom of the breastbone and belly button. This pain or discomfort comes and goes, sometimes lasting for days or weeks. The pain gets worse on an empty stomach and is relieved with food. Usually an ulcer causes pain between meals or in the middle of the night when the stomach is empty.

↪ A bloated, full feeling while eating.

↪ Loss of appetite.

↪ Weight loss.

↪ Bad breath.

↪ Nausea and/or vomiting.

Some people experience all or a few of these symptoms. Others have very mild symptoms or none at all. If left untreated, most ulcers are not life-threatening, but they can cause you misery.

Ulcer Emergency

Some ulcer symptoms require immediate medical care. Call your doctor immediately if you have:

➴ Sharp, sudden, constant stomach pain

➴ Bloody or black feces

➴ Bloody vomit or vomit that looks like coffee grounds

These symptoms could be signs that your ulcer is getting much worse. Chief among the dangers of an untreated ulcer are the following:

➴ Perforation: The ulcer has grown through the stomach or duodenal walls.

➴ Bleeding: Stomach acid or the ulcer has broken a blood vessel.

➴ Obstruction: The ulcer blocks the path of food trying to leave the stomach.

The Great Ulcer Myths

"I know why you got an ulcer," said Myles.

"What's your theory?" Tenzin asked her younger brother.

"You put hot-pepper sauce on everything. You even put it in soup and on your sandwiches. That's how you got your ulcer."

"Nope, I think it's because Tenzin is a worry-wort," said their dad. He smiled at his daughter. "You're always fretting about something."

For more than 100 years, health experts have debated the causes of ulcers. No one really knew what caused them. Because most doctors thought ulcers were caused by stress and spicy food, they advised bland diets, lots of bed rest, and stress reduction as treatment.

Other doctors believed that too much stomach acid caused ulcers. To calm painful ulcers, they recommended that people take antacids. Then in 1982, two Australian doctors discovered that a common bacteria was the culprit in most ulcer cases.

It took some time for doctors to accept this information. That is because causes and cures of health diseases are often proposed without ever being proved. Doctors want to be sure that they are correctly advising their patients with proven, accurate medical information. In 1994, however, the U.S. National Institutes of Health began to endorse, or champion, this discovery and developed a standard course of medical treatment to kill the bacteria and heal the ulcer.

Now we accept that the main cause of ulcers is bacterial infection. The second most common cause of ulcers is long-term, regular use of nonsteroidal anti-inflammatory agents (NSAIDs), such as aspirin and ibuprofen. These medicines provide pain relief from headaches and general muscle aches and are often used to treat arthritis, a chronic disease that causes inflammation and stiffness of a joint or joints in the body. NSAIDs cause ulcers by interfering with the stomach's ability to protect itself from stomach acid. In a very small number of cases, cancerous tumors in the stomach or pancreas can cause ulcers.

Ulcers are not caused by spicy foods or stress. Special diets do not help treat ulcers. So in most cases, people with ulcers can maintain a regular diet.

Understanding H. Pylori

Health experts have pinpointed the bacteria *Helicobacter pylori (H. pylori)* as the cause of most ulcers. According to the U.S. National Institute of Diabetes and Digestive and Kidney Diseases, *H. pylori* causes 80 percent of stomach ulcers and more than 90 percent of duodenal ulcers.

H. pylori infection is common in the United States. About 20 percent of those under the age of forty are infected. Half of those over the age of sixty have it. Worldwide, more than half of the population tests positive for this bacteria.

Researchers still do not know why most infected people never develop an ulcer. Infection probably depends on such things as the characteristics of the infected person, the type of *H. pylori* bacteria, and other factors that remain unknown.

How do people become infected with *H. pylori?* Researchers do not know yet. They think it may be through infected food or water. The bacteria has been found in some infected people's saliva, which means the bacteria also may be spread through mouth-to-mouth contact, such as kissing. Because *H. pylori* is not found in animals, it cannot be spread by your pet.

Researchers have learned how the bacteria does its work. Once *H. pylori* gets into a person's stomach, it thrives by secreting enzymes that neutralize stomach acid. Strong swimmers, the spiral-shaped bacteria move to the protective mucous lining of the stomach. Once there, they burrow through the mucous lining. This weakens the coating of the stomach or duodenum, and acid attacks the sensitive tissue underneath. Both the acid and the bacteria irritate the lining, resulting in an ulcer.

Once someone is infected with *H. pylori*, the bacteria will not go away without intervention. The only way to cure the infection and resulting ulcer is with medical treatment.

Diagnosing Ulcers

Dr. Mervyn suspected that Randy had an ulcer, so he had Randy go through an upper gastrointestinal (GI) series and an endoscopy. An upper GI series is an X ray of the esophagus, stomach, and duodenum. Before the X ray Randy drank a chalky, milky-white liquid containing barium. This metal causes these organs and any ulcers to show up more clearly on the X ray.

After Randy was lightly sedated with anesthesia, Dr. Mervyn carefully eased the endoscope through his nose, mouth, and throat and into the stomach and upper intestine. Noting something suspicious in Randy's stomach, Dr. Mervyn removed a tiny piece of the tissue to look at under the microscope. That's when he diagnosed Randy's ulcer.

Dr. Mervyn then tested Randy for H. pylori. He could use blood, breath, or tissue tests. He choose blood tests, which are the most common and least costly. Randy's blood was taken at Dr. Mervyn's office through a finger stick.

Some doctors still debate *H. pylori's* role in peptic ulcers, which means that some people with ulcers may not have been tested for *H. pylori* infection. The

National Institutes of Health recommends that people with an untested peptic ulcer request an *H. pylori* test from their doctor.

Healing *H. Pylori* Ulcers

"Good news, Randy. You have an ulcer," said Dr. Mervyn.

"That's lousy news," mumbled Randy.

"Well, it's bad that you have an ulcer. But here's the good part—it's caused by the H. pylori *bacteria. That means we can kill the bacteria and get rid of your ulcer. Of course it's not quite as simple as that . . ."*

Randy interrupted. "Let's get started! What do I do?"

Doctors treat *H. pylori* ulcers with a combination of three types of drugs:

⤷ Antibiotics that kill the bacteria.

⤷ Acid-suppressing drugs that reduce stomach acid, and protect the stomach lining. Two types are often used: H2 blockers and proton-pump inhibitors.

⤷ Stomach protectors, such as bismuth subsalicylate. Such medicines protect the stomach lining from stomach acid and also help kill *H. pylori*.

H2 blockers block histamine, one of three chemical messengers that signal stomach cells to churn out acid. After a few weeks, this drug will reduce Randy's stomach pain. Proton-pump inhibitors are acid reducers. They prevent all three chemical messengers from producing acid. This almost completely shuts down stomach acid production.

Doctors have prescribed H2 blockers and proton-pump inhibitors for years as ulcer treatments. However, when used alone, these drugs do not kill *H. pylori.*

Triple Treatment

Dr. Mervyn put Randy on triple treatment. For two weeks, Randy will take an acid suppressor and two antibiotics to kill the bacteria. He will be on the acid-reducing medicine longer than the antibiotics. Dr. Mervyn also could have had Randy take a stomach protector instead of the acid suppressor.

"Triple therapy is a bit tricky," Dr. Mervyn said as he handed Randy a treatment schedule. "You'll take twenty pills a day for two weeks. The antibiotics are strong. You may have some side effects from them such as nausea, vomiting, diarrhea, dark stools, dizziness, headache, and a metallic taste in your mouth."

It is difficult to kill H. pylori. *Because it lives on or in the stomach lining, the bacteria is somewhat protected from the antibiotics. For this reason Dr. Meryvn stressed,* "The only way to be sure that the drugs have killed off your infection is to take all of your medicines each day for the full two weeks, even if you're feeling better."

"Anything else?"asked Randy.

"Do you smoke?" When Randy shook his head no, Dr. Mervyn said, "Good. Smoking is particularly bad for people with ulcers. It irritates ulcers and increases stomach acid, leading to more ulcer irritation. I always recommend that anyone who uses *tobacco stop right away. You can continue to eat your regular diet because what you eat has no effect on treating your infection."*

It takes about eight weeks for most ulcers to heal completely. Once ulcer treatment is started, most people find that their ulcer pain disappears within two weeks, sometimes even in one week.

Follow-Up

After treatment, doctors do follow-up tests at four weeks and often after six months and twelve months to check for the bacteria. Results of the two-week triple therapy are impressive. In more than 90 percent of people, the bacteria is killed, ulcer symptoms are reduced or eliminated, and the ulcer never returns. A persistent infection may require a different treatment plan to kill off the bacteria.

Another option is two weeks of dual treatment. Dual treatment involves only two drugs: one antibiotic and one acid suppressor. This may be easier for some people to follow, but it is not as effective as triple therapy. Researchers are conducting studies on another treatment called quadruple therapy. This uses two antibiotics, an acid suppressor, and a stomach protector.

Treating Other Ulcers

Since most other ulcers are caused by long-term use of NSAIDs, doctors usually stop prescribing them if someone is diagnosed with an ulcer. Once the NSAIDs are stopped, most ulcers will heal. To help the healing process, doctors may recommend taking antacids to neutralize acid and H2 blockers or proton-pump inhibitors to decrease the amount of acid the stomach produces.

However, some people with arthritis must continue to take their NSAIDs. Then the doctor will prescribe regular use of H2 blockers or proton-pump inhibitors along with the NSAID.

No matter how good treatment is, some people will develop another ulcer or find that their ulcer does not heal. Or they may develop complications from their ulcer, such as bleeding. In such cases surgery may be an option.

A Future Without Ulcers

Since health experts do not yet know how *H. pylori* is spread, prevention is difficult. Researchers are working to develop a vaccine to prevent the infection.

For those who take NSAIDs and want to determine their risk of developing an ulcer, take the Ulcer Quotient (UQ) Risk Screen. This easy-to-use screening tool asks some simple questions about risk factors, including age, general health, medication use, and stomach upset while taking NSAIDs. It then calculates your UQ risk. If at high risk, you are encouraged to talk to your doctor. The UQ Risk Screen can be found online at *http://www.arthritisconnection.com.* It was developed jointly by the American Gastroenterological Association, the University of Illinois College of Medicine in Chicago, and Searle, a drug manufacturer in Chicago, Illinois.

Food Intolerances

"Let's celebrate our good scores on the math test with ice cream." Karyn opened the freezer door. "We've got chocolate chocolate chip or raspberry fudge swirl. Grab some bowls and spoons."

Karyn put the two ice-cream containers on the kitchen table. She asked, "Hey, you got out only one spoon and one bowl. What's up, Lynn?"

Odell pulled a sandwich out of his lunch bag. "Oh no, my dad's into creative cooking again."

Derek laughed as Odell inspected his sandwich. "It does look like a creation. What's in it?"

"For starters, he baked rye mustard bread. Then there's his beloved tuna-avocado-horseradish invention, sun-dried tomato, and salad dressing. Want to trade? Please?"

Derek laughed again. "I can't help you. There's only one thing I can eat out of your sandwich that I know is safe—the tomato. The rest I can't have."

Both Lynn and Odell need to avoid or restrict consuming certain foods because each has a food intolerance. Their bodies react to certain foods or a food component because they cannot digest something well. Lynn has lactose intolerance. Her body cannot digest significant amounts of lactose, the natural sugar in milk and other milk-based products. Odell cannot tolerate a protein called gluten. Gluten is found only in plant foods, specifically wheat, rye, barley, and oats.

Food Sensitivity

Do you itch when you munch on peanuts? Does eating lobster give you hives? Reactions like these can cause people to think that they are sensitive to certain foods. They may decide that they have a food allergy or a food intolerance. However, this may or may not be true.

Some people, like Lynn and Odell, have a genuine food intolerance. For metabolic reasons, their bodies cannot digest certain foods or components of certain foods. The result is uncomfortable symptoms, often targeted in the digestive system, such as bloating, gas, and diarrhea.

Other people may have a true food allergy, which causes unpleasant and sometimes serious symptoms if the particular food is consumed. In a food allergy, the body's immune system reacts when a specific food is consumed and the person develops symptoms such as upset stomach or a runny nose. In severe cases the result is anaphylactic shock, which is an acute response of the entire body—including the circulatory, respiratory, and immune systems—that if left untreated can result in death.

Unpleasant reactions to food can occur for other reasons, including infectious bacteria, parasites, or viruses, all of which can cause foodborne illnesses. Contaminants such as chemicals in the water where, for example, certain seafood is harvested, also can trigger allergy-like symptoms.

Unlike food allergies, food intolerances do not involve the immune system. However, both tend to produce many of the same symptoms, such as nausea, diarrhea, and stomach cramps. Many people tend to mislabel a food intolerance or a foodborne illness as a food allergy.

Depending on the type of food intolerance, some people can eat small amounts of the problem food and not experience unpleasant symptoms. However, someone with a food allergy cannot eat or drink any of the food and must avoid eating the problem food altogether.

Common Food Intolerances

Food intolerances usually result from a faulty metabolism. Generally symptoms occur due to poor absorption of food from the intestine into the bloodstream because the body lacks a digestive enzyme. Less often the body releases chemicals after contact with the food, causing reactions. No matter what the cause, typical food intolerance symptoms include gas, bloating, nausea, diarrhea, and stomach pain. Less common symptoms include shock; welts; fluid retention; rash; wheezing; inflamed sinuses, eyes, or nose; swelling of the vocal cords; and migraine headache.

The two most common food intolerance culprits are lactose, or milk sugar, and gluten, a protein in many edible grains. For some people, milk sugars not absorbed in the small intestine move into the large intestine. Bacteria that lives in the large intestine feeds on these sugars. As the sugars are broken down, the usual symptoms of gastric distress—bloating, gas, diarrhea, nausea, and cramps—flare up. Like those with lactose intolerance, people with gluten intolerance cannot digest a component of certain foods. In this case, the culprit is gluten.

Less Common Intolerances

Additives

"Whenever I eat Chinese food, I get a headache," Johanna says. "I think I have Chinese Restaurant Syndrome." Johanna may have an intolerance to monosodium glutamate (MSG). MSG, a flavor enhancer and additive, often is used in Chinese food. MSG is used in many types of ethnic cooking and processed foods. MSG accents the natural flavor of food and adds its own unique taste.

Various foods, medications, and cosmetics contain additives. Most of us can consume many food additives or use products containing additives without experiencing any problems. The U.S. Food and Drug Administration (FDA) regulates and sets the standards for use of food additives. Additives are used to:

- ⇨ Add nutritional value to foods. For example, B vitamins and iron are typical flour additives.

- ⇨ Enhance taste or improve the appearance of food products. Sugar and MSG are common flavor enhancers.

- ⇨ Prevent food from spoiling.

- ⇨ Give food a particular consistency so that it looks and tastes the way we expect it to be. Bottled salad dressings often contain two elements that do not mix easily—oil and water—yet stay well combined thanks to additives.

Although they provide a variety of benefits, additives can cause intolerance problems for some people. The most troublesome additives include sulfites, tartrazine, benzoates, pargenes, and various dyes, which all are used widely in foods.

Sulfites, which are the additives that people are most familiar with, prevent light-colored foods from turning brown. When added to alcoholic beverages and some foods, they slow the growth of bacteria, helping to head off foodborne illnesses. Sulfites encompass a variety of additives: sulfur dioxide, sodium sulfite, sodium bisulfite, potassium bisulfite, sodium metabisulfite, and potassium metabisulfite. Sulfites are found in many foods and beverages: dried fruits; prepared avocado dip; instant and frozen potatoes, including french fries, potato chips, dried potatoes, and potato flakes; cider; fruit juices; wine vinegar; gelatin; maraschino cherries; bottled lemon juice; salad dressings; sauces from dry mixes; shrimp; pickled products; wine; beer; and canned or dried soups.

People who are sensitive to sulfites can suffer from wheezing, diarrhea, stomachaches, hives, or swelling. Usually these symptoms are mild. But in rare instances, hypersensitive people may go into shock, especially if they're asthmatic. People with asthma are more likely to react negatively to sulfites than others. For this reason the FDA prohibits the use of sulfites on raw fruits and vegetables that will be eaten uncooked.

"Within fifteen minutes to a few hours after eating

Chinese food containing MSG, I feel tight across my face," says Johanna. Other typical, often mild symptoms of MSG intolerance include chest tightness, nausea, sweating, and a burning neck. These symptoms generally last less than an hour.

The FDA has put MSG on its list of "generally recognized as safe" foods (GRAS) for consumption. MSG intolerance is uncommon. Sometimes what people label as an MSG intolerance is actually an intolerance to something else they ate, such as the soy in soy sauce or bacteria in the food, causing a foodborne illness.

Histamine

"What do Swiss cheese, tuna casserole, and French bread have in common?"Anissa teased her friend Betti.

"They're good to eat?"

"True—except for me. They all contain histamine, a chemical that makes me sick."

Foods containing histamine sometimes can trigger symptoms. These foods include cheese, spinach, eggplant, red wine, tuna, mackerel, and yeast. The symptoms tend to mimic an allergic reaction and include headache, flushing, rapid heart rate, wheezing, and fainting. To control this, histamine-sensitive people need to avoid specific foods and beverages.

Mixed Bag

"I've sworn off sugar forever," says Rafael. "It makes me hyper. I can't seem to sit still after I eat a candy bar." Researchers are investigating whether sugar, chocolate, caffeine, and various additives can trigger headaches, make migraine headaches worse, or cause hyperactivity or attention deficit hyperactivity disorder (ADHD) in some people. This link has not been scientifically proven. Some people, though, have found relief by avoiding the foods or additives that seem to cause them problems.

Although rare, some people have an intolerance to fructose, a type of sugar found in many common foods: figs, pears, prunes, and grapes. It also is found in corn syrup, which is used to sweeten a wide array of foods and snacks, including baked goods, baked beans, jams and jellies, gums, candies, sodas, and so on. For those unable to absorb fructose, their symptoms are much like those of lactose intolerance.

"To lose weight, I switched to sugarless candy and artificial sweeteners. But I'd get awful stomachaches whenever I'd eat or drink that stuff," says Toby. To cut calories, some people turn to sugarless or diet foods, beverages, and gum. However, many will experience unpleasant GI symptoms because the sugarless ingredients are poorly absorbed by most people.

Lactose Intolerance

"You're drinking milk with your grilled-cheese sandwich? You're going to be miserable afterward." Tom shook his head.

Kevin cut his sandwich in half. "Nope. I'll be fine."

Tom started cutting cheese for his own sandwich. "So, what's your secret? I thought you were lactose intolerant."

"I am. But I've made some changes, and they're working. I can have dairy foods again."

Millions and Millions

Kevin is in good company. According to the National Institutes of Health, he is one of 30 to 50 million Americans who are lactose intolerant. These people cannot digest large amounts of lactose, the main sugar in milk. Only milk and foods made from milk are natural sources of lactose. This inability results from a shortage of the enzyme lactase. This enzyme is produced by the cells that line the small intestine. Lactase has a specific job—it breaks down milk sugar into simpler forms that can be absorbed from the small intestine into the bloodstream. When the body does not produce enough lactase to digest the lactose consumed, the results can be uncomfortable and embarrassing, as Kevin explains.

"If I get too much lactose," says Kevin, "I feel nauseated and get cramps, bloating, gas, and diarrhea. Usually this kicks in within thirty minutes to two hours after eating or drinking foods containing lactose." Kevin is describing the typical symptoms of lactose intolerance. Just how severe the symptoms are depends on the amount of lactose each person can tolerate. Not all people who are deficient in lactase have symptoms, but those who do are considered lactose intolerant.

Researchers have discovered various causes for lactose intolerance. Sometimes certain digestive diseases and injuries to the small intestine can reduce the amount of enzymes produced. Although rare, some children are born without the ability to produce lactase. For most people like Kevin, lactase deficiency develops naturally over time. After about the age of two, the cells lining the small intestine produce less and less lactase. Most people do not experience symptoms until they become adults.

Some ethnic and racial populations are more affected by lactose intolerance than others:

➥ About 50 percent of Hispanic Americans have some level of lactose intolerance.

➥ About 75 percent of all African Americans and Native Americans are lactose intolerant.

➥ Asian Americans are hit the hardest, as 90 percent are lactose intolerant.

➥ People of northern European descent tend not to have a problem with lactose intolerance.

Diagnosing Lactose Intolerance

Two years ago Kevin couldn't figure out why he had so many digestive problems. They often would start an hour or two after he ate. He set up an appointment with Dr. Applebaum.

"Kevin, we've run some tests on you, and you're as clean as a whistle!"

"Then what's going on?"

"I've got a couple of questions for you. Do you usually drink milk with your meals? Do you eat a lot of ice cream or other dairy foods every day?"

After Kevin nodded yes twice, Dr. Applebaum said, "I think you're lactose intolerant, which means that your body can't handle the milk sugar in dairy foods. Let's run a test to make sure."

Dr. Applebaum could have chosen from three medical tests: the lactose tolerance test, the hydrogen breath test, and the stool (feces) acidity test. These tests can be performed as an outpatient at a hospital, clinic, or doctor's office. For the lactose tolerance test, Kevin needed to fast before the test, then drink a sweet liquid containing lactose just before the test. Several blood samples would be taken over the next two hours to measure his blood glucose, or blood sugar level. This indicates how well his body can digest lactose. If lactose is not well broken down by the small intestine, the blood glucose level stays the same, confirming that Kevin is lactose intolerant.

The hydrogen breath test measures the amount of hydrogen in the breath. Normally, little hydrogen is in the breath. But when bacteria in the colon acts on undigested lactose, various gases, including hydrogen, are produced. The hydrogen is absorbed from the intestine into the bloodstream and carried to the lungs, where it is exhaled. So a raised level of hydrogen in the breath indicates lactose intolerance.

For young children and infants, a stool acidity test may be used. Undigested lactose will become part of the feces, which can be detected by this test.

If you suspect that you might be lactose intolerant, see your doctor. Your symptoms could be related to another digestive problem. If you are lactose intolerant, you may be surprised to find out that you can still eat dairy foods.

Enjoying Dairy Again

"You can have worse problems than being lactose intolerant," Dr. Applebaum told Kevin.

"What do you mean? I can't have milk or ice cream ever again."

"That's not true. You can control your symptoms by your diet. Most people can eat some dairy foods every day. For example, many can drink one or two glasses of milk each day. Others can manage ice cream, yogurt, and aged cheeses, like Swiss and cheddar. To find your limit, experiment. You'll have to see how much your body can handle. Some people have great success by spreading out their dairy foods over several meals."

Dr. Applebaum smiled. "Remember, lactose intolerance is not a serious health problem. You'll feel better when you eat less food with lactose or use products to help you digest lactose."

Although no cure exists, most people who are lactose intolerant can eat some dairy products regularly. Dr. Applebaum gave Kevin a sheet called "Lactose Tips." This sheet had practical ideas for dealing with lactose intolerance.

Lactose Tips

➷ Remember: Lactose is in milk and all foods made with milk, such as ice cream, ice milk, sherbet, cream, butter, cheese, cottage cheese, powdered milk, dried milk, and yogurt.

➷ Start eating small amounts of foods rich in lactose each day. Gradually increase the amount until you reach your limit.

71

⇒ Eat dairy foods with your meal, not solo. The mix of foods slows down the release of lactose into the digestive system, making it easier for your body to handle the lactose.

⇒ Spread out small amounts of lactose-rich foods during the day. Instead of drinking one glass of milk with breakfast, have a half-cup for breakfast and a half-cup for lunch.

⇒ Eat dairy foods that are lower in lactose including aged cheeses such as Swiss, colby, Parmesan, Romano, and cheddar. All of these cheeses are firm or hard. When these cheeses are made, the whey or watery liquid that forms during the cheese-making process is drained off. Most of the lactose is in the whey.

⇒ Choose yogurt and buttermilk made with active cultures. These may be easier to digest because the bacteria in these products helps digest the lactose. Not all cultured dairy foods contain live cultures. Those that do carry the National Yogurt Association's seal "Live and Active Cultures" on the carton.

⇒ Drink whole-milk dairy foods. Some people find that the higher-fat dairy products slow the rate of digestion, which slows the release of lactose.

⇒ Warning! Lactobacillus or sweet acidophilus milks contain the same amounts of lactose as regular milk.

"I think you can handle small amounts of dairy foods without problems, Kevin," Dr. Applebaum told him. "If you want to keep track of how much lactose you're taking each day, here's more information." Dr. Applebaum handed Kevin another sheet of paper.

Extreme Lactose Intolerance: Tips

- Try OTC lactase enzyme drops. To use, add a few drops to a quart of milk, stir, and refrigerate for twenty-four hours before using. The lactose level drops to 30 percent. Doubling the dose lowers the lactose level to 10 percent.

- Take chewable OTC lactase enzyme tablets or caplets just before a meal or snack. Read the directions to see how many tablets you need to take. Start with the lower dose and use more if needed.

- Buy lactose-reduced milk and other such dairy products at your supermarket. These products contain all the nutrients found in the regular products and remain fresh for about the same length of time, or longer if super-pasteurized.

- Kosher foods that display the word pareve or parve are milk-free.

- Watch out for hidden lactose. Lactose often is added to prepared foods such as creamers; bread and other baked goods; processed breakfast cereals; instant potatoes, soups, and breakfast drinks;

margarine; lunch meats; frozen meals; salad dressings; candies and other snacks; mixes for pancakes, biscuits, cookies, and scones, and so on.

➥Some products are labeled nondairy, such as coffee creamer or whipped toppings. Beware! These products may include ingredients derived from milk, and if so, they do contain lactose. If in doubt, read the ingredient label or contact the manufacturer.

➥Other words that may indicate the presence of lactose: *whey, curds, milk by-products, dry milk solids,* and *nonfat dry milk powder.*

➥More than 20 percent of prescription medicines and 6 percent of OTC medicines contain lactose. These include many types of birth control pills, stomach acid tablets, and tablets for gas. If in doubt, ask your pharmacist or doctor.

Gluten Intolerance

"Sheryl, have you been dieting? You're looking mighty thin," Duke said as he looked at his older sister.

"No, I'm not on a diet. My weight keeps dropping and I don't know why."

Duke frowned. "Are you having other problems?"

"Well, since you asked, I have a lot of gas, and my stomach bloats and sometimes hurts. I'm tired a lot too."

Soon after talking with her brother, Sheryl went to her doctor to find out if her symptoms added up to something. Here is what she found out:

"Sheryl, you have celiac disease," Dr. Jenkins told her. "This digestive disease damages the small intestine and interferes with absorption of nutrients from food. The culprit is gluten, which is found in wheat, rye, barley, and oats."

"Ohmigosh! That's a lot of stuff." Sheryl slumped in her chair.

"Yes, you will always have to be careful of what you eat. We'll talk more about that. First, here's what is happening to you when you eat foods containing gluten. Celiac disease is actually an autoimmune disease—this means your body's immune system causes the damage to your small intestine. It is also a digestive disease, one of malabsorption, because nutrients from foods are not absorbed. No matter what you eat or how much you eat, your small intestine has been damaged, you aren't getting the nutrients you need, and you've become malnourished. That's why you're losing weight and feeling tired."

A Long History

Celiac disease has been known for more than 2,000 years. Over the centuries some people discovered that by eliminating wheat from their diet, they felt better. Compared to other grains, wheat contains the most gluten. Today researchers know that gluten intolerance stems from the body's inability to tolerate gluten, the protein component in some grains and edible grasses. Once consumed, gluten breaks down into two parts, gliadin and glutenin. Gliadin is the actual culprit in celiac disease.

Gliadin damages the lining of the small intestine. If someone with celiac disease continues to eat wheat products, the damaged intestine no longer can absorb essential nutrients such as proteins, carbohydrates, fats, and fat-soluble vitamins—the building blocks of cells.

Celiac disease goes by other names, including celiac sprue, nontropical sprue, and gluten-sensitive enteropathy. Because it runs in families, celiac disease is a genetic disease. Sometimes this disease is triggered, or becomes active for the first time, due to a major event such as surgery, pregnancy, childbirth, viral infection, or severe emotional stress.

How Rare?

The National Institute of Diabetes and Digestive and Kidney Diseases (NIDDK) estimates that 1 in 4,700 Americans has been diagnosed with celiac disease. Yet this estimate is questionable. The NIDDK suggests that this figure could be much higher, as high as 1 in every 250 people. Why the discrepancy?

Celiac disease is the most common genetic disease in Europe. For example, in Italy about 1 in 250 people have it. In Ireland the rate is 1 in 300 people. However, celiac disease is seldom found in African, Chinese, and Japanese people. Since so many Americans are descended from European ethnic groups, researchers believe that celiac disease is underdiagnosed in the United States. Part of the problem is that many American doctors are not knowledgeable about the disease, and few American laboratories are experienced and skilled at testing for celiac disease.

In addition, celiac disease affects people differently.

Sometimes the disease shows up in children. Others, though, may not be diagnosed until they are forty or older.

What It Feels Like

Sometimes the symptoms of celiac disease don't appear in the digestive system. LaPhonso recalled, "Before I found out that I had celiac disease, I'd feel irritable and depressed." One of the most common symptoms in children is irritability. Other people with the disease may have diarrhea and stomach pain. Someone may have just one or quite a few of the symptoms. Here are the typical symptoms of celiac disease:

- Recurring stomach bloating and pain

- Constant diarrhea

- Unexplained weight loss

- Pale, bad-smelling feces

- Anemia, or low red blood cell count

- Gas

- Bone pain

- Behavior changes, such as depression or irritability

- Muscle cramps

- Fatigue

- Delayed growth, failure to thrive

☞ Joint pain

☞ Seizures or convulsions because of inadequate absorption of folic acid, a B vitamin. (Lack of folic acid causes calcium deposits to form in the brain, which can cause seizures.)

☞ Tingling numbness in the legs due to nerve damage

☞ Pale sores inside the mouth

☞ Painful skin rash

☞ Tooth discoloration or loss of tooth enamel

☞ Missed menstrual periods due to excessive weight loss

Many of these symptoms, such as delayed growth, anemia, and weight loss, are signs of malnutrition, or not getting enough nutrients from foods. Malnutrition is a particularly serious problem for children and teens because they need good nutrition to grow and develop properly.

If left untreated the small intestine will become further damaged, and the continual malnutrition can lead to serious health problems. Celiac disease puts people at risk for developing several types of intestinal cancers and osteoporosis. Osteoporosis, resulting from poor calcium absorption, is a condition in which the bones become weak, brittle, and prone to breaking. A pregnant woman with celiac disease could miscarry her baby, or the baby could be born with nerve damage. Children with untreated celiac disease often do not grow as tall as they would if they were in good health. Yet if the disease is diagnosed and treated before their growth period stops, these children will catch up on their growth.

Diagnosing and Screening

At first, Carla's doctor was not sure what to make of her symptoms. After Dr. Milton ruled out an assortment of possible problems, she decided to test for celiac disease. People with celiac disease have higher than normal levels of certain antibodies in their blood. Antibodies are produced by the immune system in response to substances that the body sees as threatening. To diagnose celiac disease, Dr. Milton tested Carla's blood to measure levels of antibodies to gluten.

After the test came back positive, Dr. Milton needed to assess the level of damage in Carla's small intestine. So she scheduled Carla for a biopsy. During this procedure the doctor removes a tiny piece of tissue from the small intestine and examines it under a microscope. The actual procedure is done by easing a long, thin tube called an endoscope through the nose, mouth, and stomach into the small intestine. Once the end of the tube is positioned, the doctor takes tiny samples. Biopsy is the only sure way to diagnose celiac disease.

After Carla's biopsy came back positive, Dr. Milton recommended that Carla's parents and brother be screened for the disease. "Screening is smart," she explained, "even though your parents and Simon show no signs of the disease. Screening involves the same blood test you went through."

Carla wrinkled her forehead. "If no one else in my family shows symptoms, why bother with screening?"

"Celiac disease is hereditary. That means family members, especially first-degree relatives, are at higher risk for having the disease. About 10 percent of your relatives—parents, brothers, and sisters—will also have the disease. The sooner we can diagnose celiac disease, the sooner we can start treatment, and the sooner we head off trouble. By the way, if you have kids, they'll need to be screened for celiac disease, too."

The Only Sure Way

Carla listened to Dr. Milton. Then she asked, "So what pills do I need to take? For how long?"

"Whoa!" Dr. Milton smiled. "There's only one treatment for celiac disease: a gluten-free diet. You no longer can have any foods that contain gluten. If you eat a completely gluten-free diet, your symptoms will stop, your small intestine will heal, and you'll prevent further damage to your digestive system."

"How soon will I notice anything?"

"Fast! Within days of starting your new diet, you'll feel better because your symptoms will begin to subside. It can take three to six months to heal your small intestine. Actually, you're lucky. For older adults, it can take up to two years before they are healed."

A gluten-free diet is tough to follow. Dr. Milton told Carla, "You must stick to your gluten-free diet for the rest of your life. You can't share a pizza with friends or eat a store-bought birthday cake ever again. Eating any gluten, no matter how small an amount, will damage your intestine and make you feel miserable."

A small number of people with celiac disease won't improve on a gluten-free diet. For example, if they have had tooth discoloration or delayed growth, these problems may not go away. For others, the disease may have severely damaged their intestines to such an extent that they may need nutrition supplements. Researchers are investigating medicines to help these people.

No More Pizza?

Carla asked Dr. Milton, "So what can I eat, and what do I avoid?"

"In two sentences, avoid all foods that contain wheat—that includes spelt, triticale, and kamut— plus rye, barley, oats, millet, and buckwheat. That translates into most grains, breads, cereals, pasta, and many processed foods."

Carla shuddered. "What's left to eat?"

"You'll be surprised. Once you get used to your diet, you will find that you can eat a variety of foods. You'll need to be creative and adventurous at times. For example, instead of wheat flour, substitute other flours such as potato, soy, rice, or bean. Some food companies sell a variety of gluten-free bread, pasta, and other foods. You can make gluten-free bread yourself. And don't forget that you can eat plain rice, meat, fish, fruits, and vegetables."

Most people find that it takes time to adjust to all the dietary changes. It's complicated, requiring that you

take a new approach to eating. You can't grab anything for lunch at the school cafeteria. Going for pizza
after a movie is out. In fact, eating out becomes chal-
lenging, especially at first when you're trying to
remember all the restrictions. But you learn to scruti-
nize the menu for foods with gluten and to question
your waiter or chef about possible hidden sources.
After a while, screening for gluten becomes a habit.

Dr. Milton gave Carla a list of allowed foods and
foods to avoid for her nongluten diet. "This list is not
complete. If you have questions, ask me or a dietitian
who specializes in celiac disease. A dietitian is a health
care professional who specializes in food and nutrition."

The doctor added, "Label reading will become a
way of life for you." She handed Carla another sheet
of paper. "Here's a list of ingredients found on many
food labels that signal the use of gliadin or gluten.
Watch out for anything that contains flour, modified
food starch, monosodium glutamate (MSG),
hydrolyzed vegetable protein (HVP), cereals, malt
extract, cereal extract, malt flavoring, distilled vinegar, emulsifiers, stabilizers, or wheat starch."

Back to Health

Although somewhat daunting at first, a gluten-free diet will
bring great relief. Without gliadin in the diet, people with
gluten intolerance will heal and can live long, healthy lives.

The Uncommon
Food Allergy

"I'll pass." Sara shook her head.
"But I made this pecan pie for you," said her mother.
"I think I'm allergic to pecans. Remember when you made that fudge cake with pecans? That's when I first thought I had developed an allergy to nuts."

Have you heard people say that they have a food allergy? Perhaps you avoid a particular food thinking that you are allergic to it. Although many people—almost one out of four—think that they have a food allergy, most have given themselves the wrong diagnosis.

The fact is, about 1 percent or less of adult Americans have a true allergy to food. Food allergies are more common in children. The National Institute of Allergy and Infectious Diseases says that about 3 percent of children under the age of three have medically proven allergic reactions to food. Many children outgrow their allergies by the time they become teens.

Allergy Claims

If food allergies are uncommon, why do so many people claim that they are allergic to certain foods? Most people self-diagnose, that is, they decide that they have an allergy without consulting a doctor to see if this is, in fact, the case. In most cases they don't. In addition, the symptoms they may experience can mimic other food-induced problems, such as foodborne illnesses or food intolerances. People often use the term allergy incorrectly to refer to almost any physical reaction to food.

If you react to food but don't have an allergy, you may have a food intolerance. Food intolerance reactions are usually temporary and seldom life-threatening. Unlike food allergies, food intolerances involve problems with digestion, or the breakdown of foods.

Haywire Immune Response

An allergic reaction is how the body responds to an irritating and potentially harmful substance. With a food allergy, the body's immune system reacts to certain substances in some foods. These substances, usually proteins, are called allergens.

Experts do not yet know why the immune system sees these allergens as an enemy. But when a particular food is eaten by someone with a food allergy, the immune system responds to allergens in the same way it does with foreign invaders. In other words, it sees that food substance as something to be destroyed.

To fight off the allergen, the body produces antibodies. These antibodies cause the body to release certain chemicals, such as histamine. Once these chemicals are carried throughout the body by the bloodstream, they trigger allergy symptoms: a runny nose, itching, swelling in the lips or mouth, or a faster heartbeat.

The Culprits

"What's happening to your mouth?" Kyle's right eyebrow shot up, a sure sign he was worried.

"What do you mean? My lips feel funny." Jeremy headed for the bathroom.

Kyle followed him. "You must be allergic to something we just ate."

Jeremy touched his swollen lip. "I've never had problems eating shrimp fried rice before. This is weird."

Like Jeremy, people of any age can develop allergies to foods that never bothered them before. Even a single episode can spell trouble: Some allergies can cause what is called anaphylaxis, which is a sudden, severe, and sometimes life-threatening allergic reaction. Most food allergies develop during childhood. The tendency toward developing them seems to be inherited—passed down in the genes from a parent to a child. Heredity may cause a predisposition—or an increased risk of—developing a food allergy. Most people with food allergies are allergic to three or fewer foods.

Some foods are more likely than others to trigger an allergic reaction, depending on the age of the person. In adults the top four are tree nuts, such as cashews, pecans, hazelnuts, walnuts, and almonds; peanuts (they're legumes, not nuts); shrimp and other shellfish; and regular fish. These account for most "real" food allergies. Other culprits include foods that contain milk, soy, or wheat. Adults seldom lose their food allergies.

For children the food culprits are somewhat different. The most common are eggs, milk, and peanuts. Luckily if kids have a food allergy, it is usually to only one or two foods. Also, most children outgrow their food allergies within a few years. They are more likely to outgrow allergies to milk or soy as opposed to allergies to nuts, peanuts, fish, or shrimp. In fact, allergies to peanuts and tree nuts are considered lifelong.

"I think I'm allergic to food dyes," says Robyn. Like Robyn, some people blame chemical additives in food—such as preservatives, sulfites, MSG, and dyes—when their tummy gurgles and moans after they eat certain foods. However, most true food allergies involve a reaction to proteins. Very few people have an allergy to food additives, however, of these people, a small percentage have an allergy to sulfite additives. By FDA law, sulfite-containing foods and beverages must be labeled.

Combination Allergies

People with food allergies may have cross-sensitivity. When Jeremy discovered he had an allergy to shrimp, his doctor checked him for allergies to other shellfish, such as crab and lobster. "It turned out that I'm allergic to all shellfish," says Jeremy. "My doctor said that's called cross-reactivity."

Bonita has another type of cross sensitivity. "I'm miserable during ragweed pollination season. My nose and eyes run constantly. What's weird is that when my ragweed allergy is really bad, I can't eat melons, especially cantaloupe. If I try to eat these fruits, my mouth itches badly." Sometimes people with a severe birch pollen allergy will have a similar allergic reaction if they eat apple peel.

Misery of Food Allergies

"Want a bite?" Sandy offered his candy bar to Montel.

Don pushed the candy away from his brother. "Don't eat that, Montel! Sandy, take that outside, now!"

Sandy ran out the front door. He soon heard Don running after him. "Sorry to be rude."

The two friends looked at each other. "I'm not some sleaze offering bad candy to your little brother," said Sandy.

"I know. It's just that Montel is very allergic to peanuts. He gets hives, swells up, and sneezes a lot from touching or even smelling anything containing peanuts. One time he had a lot of trouble breathing and nearly died. I didn't want to take any chances."

Not all allergies trigger such severe reactions as Montel's. The severity depends on how allergic the person is to the particular food. Most people with a food allergy know right away that they are having a reaction if they have consumed the wrong food. Generally symptoms set in within a few to forty-five minutes after eating the problem food.

That response is quite different from what someone with a food intolerance experiences. Don has lactose intolerance. "My symptoms usually start a couple hours after I eat a lot of pizza or ice cream," he explains.

Food intolerances and food allergies differ in another way. Food intolerance symptoms generally target—and are limited to—the digestive system. Don explains, "If I eat too many dairy foods, I get stomach cramps, bloating, diarrhea, and gas. Sometimes I'll even vomit." But food allergy symptoms typically cause reactions in many different parts of the body, including the digestive system, mouth, airways, and skin. Typical food allergy symptoms include the following:

➭ Fatigue.

➭ Swelling of the lips or tongue, itchy lips.

➭ Chronic crying and spitting up in infants.

➭ Headache, including migraine.

➭ Aches and pains in arms and legs or joints.

➭ Anxiety.

➭ Behavioral problems in children.

➭ Vaginal discharge.

➭ Fluid retention.

➭ Runny and/or stuffy nose, sneezing.

➭ Skin problems including eczema (skin becomes red, scaly and itchy), hives, rash, and dry and flaky skin.

➭ Diarrhea and/or constipation, excessive gas, bloating, nausea, and stomach pain or cramps.

➭ Breathing difficulties ranging from shortness of breath to wheezing or asthma.

➭ Seizures.

↪ Anaphylaxis, which is a rare but potentially fatal condition wherein the immune, circulatory, and respiratory systems react simultaneously. It can cause respiratory distress, shock, and even death.

Potentially Fatal

Anaphylaxis occurs fast, within minutes of being exposed to the problem food. Don remembers when his little brother, Montel, had a violent allergic reaction to peanuts.

"Just minutes after Montel had taken a bite of his peanut butter sandwich, big red bumps started popping out all over his body. My mom said they were hives. Montel kept scratching them even though he was not supposed to. Then his throat swelled up, and I could hear that he was having trouble breathing. When my mom, who's a nurse, checked him over, she said that his blood pressure had dropped. She told me to call 911, which I did. Luckily Montel was okay afterward."

People who go into anaphylactic shock can become unconscious and even die if not treated immediately. According to the National Food Allergy Network, about 125 people die each year from anaphylaxis. Fortunately most food-allergic people never have an anaphylactic reaction.

Any food can trigger anaphylaxis, but the problem arises most commonly from peanuts, tree nuts, shellfish, milk, eggs, or fish. All it takes is one-fifth to one-five-thousandth of a teaspoon of the culprit food to cause death. Anaphylaxis seldom occurs the first time someone eats a particular food. Currently no specific test exists to predict the likelihood of anaphylaxis.

Anaphylaxis can produce severe symptoms in five to fifteen minutes. However, life-threatening reactions can progress over hours. The sooner anaphylaxis is treated, the greater the person's chance of surviving. A person experiencing an anaphylactic reaction needs to get to a hospital emergency room as soon as possible, even if the symptoms seem to be subsiding.

Don't Play Doctor

Think you have a food allergy? See a board-certified allergist to get an accurate diagnosis. A board-certified allergist is a medical doctor who is certified by the American Board of Allergy and Immunology. Someone with a food allergy should be under a doctor's care.

Be careful of diagnosing yourself with a food allergy. Instead of an allergy, you may have an intolerance to a food or additive. You may have jumped to a wrong conclusion and instead have another digestive problem that needs to be diagnosed and treated by a physician. Eliminating eggs, milk, or nuts from your diet because you suspect a food allergy is not a good idea. You may be denying yourself important nutrients and the fun of eating a variety of foods based on an inaccurate self-diagnosis.

Allergy Hunting

Diane told her doctor, "I think I'm allergic to eggs."
"We'll have to assess several things to see if you do

have a food allergy," Dr. Chin said. He held up three fingers. "First I'll take your history; then I'll have you do a diet diary and an elimination diet." After Dr. Chin grabbed a notepad and pen, he asked Diane a series of questions:

☞How fast did your reaction come on—within an hour or less after eating the food?

☞What actually happened during your reaction? What were your symptoms?

☞Did you get any treatment? If so, was it allergy treatment? Was the treatment successful? (For example, antihistamines will relieve many allergy symptoms, such as hives and itching.)

☞Does the reaction always occur when you eat a certain food?

☞Did any other people get sick when they ate the same food you did? (If it's an allergic reaction, only someone with an allergy will get sick. Everyone else will feel fine.)

☞How much did you eat before experiencing a reaction?

☞How was the food prepared? (Some people will have a violent allergic reaction to a particular food only if it is raw or undercooked.)

☞Were other foods eaten at the time of the allergic reaction? (Because some foods may delay digestion, they also may delay how soon the allergic reaction began.)

⮑ Does anyone else in the family have allergies or food allergies?

Dr. Chin asked Diane to keep a diet diary for a week. Diane will record all food, beverages, and medicines she consumes over this time period and her reactions, if any, to them. A diet diary helps the doctor determine if there is a consistency in the reactions. Not all doctors will request a diet diary.

After Diane completed the diet diary, Dr. Chin had her follow an elimination diet. Not all doctors will require this step. Under the doctor's direction, the person stops eating the food or foods suspected of causing the allergy. In Diane's case, she could not eat eggs of any kind, even eggs in baked goods such as cookies or cake. If, under Dr. Chin's direction, Diane re-introduces eggs into her diet and the symptoms return, a strong probability exists that she is allergic to eggs. An elimination diet will not work as a diagnostic tool if Diane's reactions to the food are severe or infrequent.

The Hunt Continues

If the food history, diet diary, and elimination diet point to a specific food allergy, the doctor then will use medical tests to measure the allergic response to the food. Dr. Chin did a scratch skin test on Diane. He placed a dilute, or weak, extract of the food on the skin of her forearm. (He also could have placed the extract on her back.) Then he gently scratched a portion of the skin with a needle so that a tiny amount entered the skin. If the skin swells or turns red, this indicates an allergic reaction.

Skin tests are generally fast, simple, and safe. However, a person can have a positive skin test to a food without experiencing allergic reactions to that food. A diagnosis of a food allergy is made only when:

- The person has a positive skin test to a specific food.

- The history of the reactions suggests an allergy to the same food.

"I'm very allergic to nuts. My doctor couldn't do skin tests on me because I could have had a dangerous reaction," recalls Roger. "So he ran a blood test."

Blood tests measure the presence of food-specific antibodies in the blood. The drawbacks of these tests are that they cost more than skin tests, and the results take a week or more to come back from the laboratory. As with skin testing, positive tests do not automatically provide a diagnosis.

The most accurate food allergy test is called a blind or double-blind challenge test. In a blind challenge test, the patient is given either a capsule of the food without being told what it is, or a placebo, which is a similar capsule containing an inert, or nonreacting, substance. The placebo is the control in the test. In this type of test, the doctor knows what substance the patient has taken. During the test the patient and doctor record any symptoms of allergic reaction. In a double-blind challenge test, both the patient and doctor do not know if the person is given the food or the placebo.

Challenge tests work well, but they are not used very often. For one thing, they do not work for someone with a severe allergic reaction to a food. Also, this testing is costly because it takes a lot of time to conduct. Finally, multiple food allergies are difficult to evaluate with this method.

Medications for Food Allergies

Unfortunately no medication exists to prevent food allergies. You can take several medications to relieve mild food allergy symptoms. Antihistamines will relieve digestive upset, hives, or sneezing and a runny nose. Bronchodilators can help with breathing problems.

"I try to avoid anything with seafood, since I'm mildly allergic to shrimp, crab, lobster, and so on. But if I somehow eat these foods and can feel my symptoms kicking in, I take antihistamines. Within ten to fifteen minutes, my nose stops running, and my itching and hives calm down," says Derek.

These medications are taken after someone has accidentally consumed an allergy-provoking food. However, they cannot prevent an allergic reaction from occurring in the first place. So the only treatment is to avoid the specific food completely. That may not be as easy as it sounds.

Reading Labels

Joan says, "Because of my wheat allergy, I can't eat my favorites—pizza, pasta, bread, crackers, cookies, and cake. Then I began to read the labels on all prepared foods. I couldn't believe how often wheat and wheat products are added. Anything with a sauce is a no-no, for example."

Leroy got help from a registered dietitian for his peanut allergy. "Other than not eating peanut butter *and peanut candy, I wasn't sure what else to avoid. The dietitian helped me learn to manage my food allergy and showed me that I still could eat a varied, balanced diet. She also taught me how to read food labels.*

"I'm now pretty good at reading food labels," he continues. "I'm also allergic to eggs, and I found out that they are used in some foods I'd never have thought about, such as mayonnaise, salad dressings, and ice cream."

Food labels, by FDA law, must list the ingredients in packaged foods. However, manufacturers have to list only those ingredients that make up 2 percent or more of the product. Leroy explains, "If I'm in doubt, I don't take a chance; I call the manufacturer to check on exactly what's in the product." Many companies list their names, addresses, and toll-free telephone numbers on packaging.

Stephen learned the hard way that sometimes labels don't tell all. "I thought that certain chocolate candies were safe for me even though I have a peanut allergy, but I got sick from eating them. After a phone call, I discovered that many times machines or vats that make a non-peanut candy also are used to make a peanut candy."

Food labels change, so it is important to read them regularly. Jolene notes, "A few months ago, I couldn't eat a certain brand of chips because the product contained peanut oil, and I'm allergic to peanuts. Then the company switched to corn oil!"

Other Strategies

Cathy likes to cook and bake. "Once my egg allergy was confirmed, I started to experiment. I've found that I often can substitute one food for another and get great results. For instance, instead of eggs in my cakes and muffins, I use applesauce."

Another tip is to clean carefully all cutting boards or counters soiled by foods that can trigger your allergy. Always use clean utensils and plates. By taking these steps, you can head off a possible allergic reaction.

Tracy had a surprise allergic reaction when she ate a vanilla ice cream cone. "I'm allergic to nuts and always avoid them. A few weeks ago, I ordered a vanilla ice cream cone. I thought that I was safe with vanilla. But the clerk used a scoop that contained traces of a nut-containing ice cream to make my cone. I had a nasty reaction." As Tracy found out, cross-contamination during preparation of foods can occur.

Eating with a food allergy can be tricky sometimes. Always read food labels. If you do eat out, ask the waiter or chef about the ingredients and preparation of foods before you order them. If in doubt, avoid the food. As an alternative to eating out, pack yourself a tasty take-along meal.

Being Prepared

For most people with food allergies, symptoms are unpleasant but not serious. However, a small number of people can have an anaphylactic reaction. Janie once had an anaphylactic reaction to peanuts. Since then she has taken precautions. "I wear an identification bracelet or necklace to let others know of my allergy. I also carry an EpiPen. It's a syringelike device that delivers a shot of epinephrine to keep my heart going in case I have a severe reaction."

Epinephrine, or adrenaline, is a man-made version of a naturally occurring hormone. To treat an anaphylactic reaction, it is injected into the skin, usually in the thigh. It works directly on the cardiovascular (heart and blood vessels) and respiratory (lungs and airways) systems. Adrenaline quickly constricts the blood vessels, reverses throat swelling, relaxes the lungs to improve breathing, and stimulates the heartbeat.

Carrie calls her EpiPen a "fat pen." She says, "I've used it twice to prevent myself from going into shock. When I feel my throat swelling and I have trouble breathing, I know I'm having a bad reaction. So I remove the safety cap on my EpiPen and push the automatic injector tip against my outer thigh. I hold the EpiPen in place for a few seconds so that all the adrenaline goes in; then I throw it away."

The EpiPen delivers one premeasured dose of epinephrine. An Ana-Kit, which is a needle and syringe kit, provides two doses. Which system someone uses is a decision made by the doctor and the person.

If you or someone else experiences a severe food allergy reaction, call 911 or an ambulance right away. If the person has an EpiPen or Ana-Kit, use it at the first sign of an anaphylactic reaction. The medication is most effective when followed by immediate medical treatment. That's because it provides only about fifteen minutes of relief, usually enough time for the emergency team to arrive and get the person to a hospital for further treatment, if needed.

The Future

The National Institutes of Health supports research on food allergies through grants that it provides to research organizations throughout the world. Researchers are now working to better understand the cause of the immune system dysfunction in allergies. This helps them develop better methods of diagnosing, treating, and preventing allergic diseases.

St. Margaret Middle School Library
1716-A Churchville Road
Bel Air, Maryland 21015

Take Time to Digest

What is the best way to care for your digestive system? The answer is to treat your body well. As an extra benefit, this will help you look and feel good.

The three key components of caring for your digestive system are eating well, keeping fit, and managing stress. Combined, they add up to overall good health. Three factors play an important role in each of these areas: variety, moderation, and balance. For example, by eating less high-fat foods, you'll make room for more vegetables and fruits in your diet. Or by watching less television every day, you will find more time to do fun, relaxing activities such as enjoying a hobby or being with your friends.

The bottom line is that you can control much of your own comfort and well-being. You can head off many digestive problems with some simple techniques or a bit of planning. If you have a digestive disease, you may need to take medications and work with health professionals. Even so, the information in the remaining chapters will help get you started in caring for your digestive system and being good to yourself.

Eating Well

Good eating habits are often the best way to avoid or lessen stomach problems. Many digestive disorders respond well to diet improvements. For example, eating plenty of high-fiber foods can help relieve constipation or diarrhea.

We all need about forty nutrients, or basic dietary components, to stay healthy. Nutrients are substances in food that the body needs to grow, repair itself, and supply itself with energy. Basic nutrients include minerals, vitamins, carbohydrates, proteins, fats, and water. No one food has all forty nutrients in adequate amounts needed for growth, energy, and good health. That is why eating a variety of foods each day is so important. That way, your body gets the many nutrients it needs.

Minerals

Minerals, which are inorganic substances that come from foods, help regulate many of the body's processes. Although they make up about 4 percent of your weight, minerals are essential to your life. They help regulate many processes that take place in your body, such as fluid balance, muscle contractions, and nerve impulses. Without minerals you could not chew your food (you would not have any teeth) or stand (because you would not have bones). Minerals are found in teeth, muscles, blood, and other body tissues.

By eating a balanced diet, one with lots of different foods, you will get an abundant amount of most minerals. The two mineral deficiencies that most often show up in teens, especially during periods of rapid growth, are deficiencies of iron and calcium. That is because your iron needs are highest during your teens. And your bones take in the most calcium during the teen years and early twenties, when you are still growing.

Can you name the fifteen minerals that your body needs for good health? Here they are:

Major Minerals

The major minerals are those that the body requires in daily amounts of more than 250 milligrams. Listed below are the names of these minerals, the recommended minimum daily amount for good health (in parentheses), what use the body makes of each of these substances, and food sources that contain these minerals.

➤ Calcium (1,200 mg.) builds bone, keeps bones strong, helps muscles contract and your heart beat, regulates nerve function, and aids blood clotting. It can be found in dairy products, dark green leafy vegetables, fish with edible bones, calcium-fortified foods, and tofu made with calcium sulfate.

➤ Chloride (750 mg.) helps regulate cell fluids and gastric juices and transmits nerve impulses. The best source of chloride is common table salt, which is made of sodium and chloride. One-quarter teaspoon of salt contains 750 mg. of chloride.

➤ Magnesium (280-350 mg.) aids in bone growth and muscle contraction and is used in more than 300 body enzymes that regulate body functions. It can be found in most foods; the best sources are legumes, nuts, whole grains, and green vegetables.

➤ Phosphorus (1,200 mg.) is essential in cell metabolism and to the development and maintenance of the bones and teeth. It also maintains acid-base balance in blood. It is found in most foods, with the best sources being protein-rich foods such as milk, meat, poultry, fish, eggs, legumes, and nuts.

⮑Potassium (2,000 mg.) regulates fluids and mineral balance in cells, maintains blood pressure, transmits nerve impulses, and helps muscles contract. It is found in most foods; the best sources are fruits, many vegetables, fresh meat, poultry, and fish.

⮑Sodium (2,400 mg.) regulates fluids and mineral balance in cells, maintains blood pressure, transmits nerve impulses, and helps muscles relax. The best sources are processed foods, sauces, and table salt.

Trace Minerals
Trace minerals are elements that the body also needs for good health, although in lesser amounts than the major minerals:

⮑Chromium (50–200 mg.) works with insulin to help your body use glucose, or blood sugar. It can be found in meat, poultry, eggs, whole grains, cheese, or peas.

⮑Copper (1.5–3.0 mg.) helps make hemoglobin in many body enzymes. It can be found in organ meats, seafood and fish, and nuts and seeds.

⮑Fluorine (1.5–2.5 mg.) helps harden tooth enamel and strengthen bones. It is not widely available in food except in tea and fish with edible bones.

⮑Iodine (150–mg.) is part of a thyroid hormone that regulates the rate at which your body uses energy.

It can be found in iodized table salt and saltwater fish. A half-teaspoon of iodized salt contains almost 150 mg of iodine.

☙ Iron (10–15 mg.) is an essential part of hemoglobin, which carries oxygen to every body cell. It can be found in meats, seafood, poultry, legumes, dried fruits, egg yolks, fortified foods, and enriched rice.

☙ Manganese (2–5 mg.) is part of many enzymes; good sources are whole grains, tea, nuts, green leafy vegetables, and legumes.

☙ Molybdenum (75–250 mg.) is part of many enzymes and helps turn iron into hemoglobin to make red blood cells; sources are milk, legumes, breads, and whole grains.

☙ Selenium (55–70 mg.) works with vitamin E to protect cells from damage. It can be found in seafood, liver, kidneys, and whole grains.

☙ Zinc (12–15 mg.) is essential for cell reproduction and tissue growth and repair, and it is part of more than seventy enzymes. Good sources are meat, seafood, liver, eggs, and milk.

Vitamins

Vitamins are compounds that help regulate many body processes, such as digestion, absorption, and metabolism. Your body can manufacture two vitamins: vitamin D if exposed to sunlight and vitamin K from bacteria in your intestines. The others come from the foods you eat. Here's the scoop on vitamins:

➥ Vitamin A (800–1,000 retinol equivalents, or REs) helps you see in the dark; aids in growth and health of bones, cells and tissues; and possibly aids in cancer prevention. It can be found in dairy products; red, orange, yellow, and green vegetables; orange fruits; liver; eggs; and vitamin A-fortified foods.

➥ Vitamin D (400 International Units, or IUs) helps absorb calcium and phosphorus for growth and health of bones and teeth. Good sources are fortified milk and other dairy products, eggs, fortified foods, and salmon. Vitamin D is produced by the skin when exposed sunlight.

➥ Vitamin E (8–10 mgs.) may protect against some diseases. It can be found in vegetable oils, margarine, salad dressings, nuts, seeds, and wheat germ.

➥ Vitamin K (65–80 micrograms) is essential in blood clotting and helps maintain blood calcium levels. The best sources are green leafy vegetables, especially spinach and broccoli; eggs; liver; and tomatoes. It also is produced by intestinal bacteria.

➥ Vitamin B_1 (1.1–1.5 mgs.) also is known as thiamin. It changes glucose into energy or fat. Good sources are whole grain and enriched grain products, pork, and organ meats.

➥ Vitamin B_2 (1.3–1.7 mgs.) also is known as

riboflavin. It helps produce energy from foods and keeps skin healthy. Good sources are dairy foods, organ meats, enriched grain products, eggs, meat, and green leafy vegetables.

↪ Niacin (15–19 mgs.) helps in energy production and the maintenance of body tissue. Best sources are foods high in protein, such as poultry, fish, beef, peanut butter, legumes, and enriched/fortified grain products.

↪ Vitamin B_6 (1.6–2.0 mgs.) is essential to amino acid and carbohydrate metabolism. Good sources are chicken, fish, pork, liver, kidneys, whole grain products, nuts, and legumes.

↪ Folic acid (180–200 micrograms) is also known as folate. It is essential in making new body cells and helps form hemoglobin. Good sources are legumes, nuts, liver, leafy vegetables, orange juice, and folic-enriched grain products.

↪ Vitamin B_{12} (2.0 micrograms) helps make red blood cells and is necessary for normal growth. It can be found mostly in animal products—meat, fish, poultry, eggs, and dairy foods—and in some fortified foods.

↪ Biotin (30–100 micrograms) helps metabolize proteins, fats, and carbohydrates from your food. It can be found in many foods, especially eggs, liver, yeast breads, and cereals.

↪ Panthothenic acid (4–7 mgs.) helps metabolize

proteins, fats, and carbohydrates from your food. It is found in most foods, especially meat, poultry, fish, whole grains, and legumes.

↝ Vitamin C (60 mgs.) is also known as ascorbic acid. It protects against infection, helps form connective tissue, helps wounds heal, maintains blood vessels, and helps keep gums and teeth healthy. Good sources are citrus fruits such as oranges, lemons, grapefruit, limes, and tangerines; berries; melons; peppers; green vegetables; tomatoes; cabbage; and potatoes.

Carbohydrates

What is a carbohydrate? Think of sugar, starch, and fiber. All are the body's preferred source of energy, or calories. In fact, health experts recommend that 55 to 60 percent of your calories come from carbohydrates, especially complex carbohydrates such as whole grains, legumes, seeds, nuts, and potatoes and other vegetables.

Dietary fiber is another type of complex carbohydrate. You can see fiber in some vegetables, grains, and fruits. It's tough and stringy and not digestible. Fiber helps move waste through your digestive system and helps prevent many problems, such as constipation and diarrhea.

Simple carbohydrates, also called sugars, are present in many foods such as fruits, some vegetables, and milk. One type of sugar, though, is best eaten sparingly. That is processed sugar, the white or brown sugar that comes in bags or boxes. Other processed sugars are corn syrups and molasses. Processed sugar is a large part of desserts, candies, and soft drinks.

"But aren't carbohydrates fattening?" asks Sheila. No. One ounce of a carbohydrate has the same number of calories as a protein, but less calories than an ounce of fat.

Proteins

Proteins, which are made of chains of building blocks called amino acids, are found in every body cell. Their main role is to build, repair, and maintain all body cells and tissues. Proteins in enzymes, hormones, and antibodies also help regulate many body processes. Hormones regulate reactions.

About 10 to 15 percent of your diet should come from protein. Good sources of protein include fish, poultry, meat, eggs, most dairy products, legumes, nuts, and seeds. Some vegetables and whole grains supply smaller amounts of protein.

Fats

"With all the talk about how bad fats are, why should I eat them?" Trevor wonders. Fats are an important part of your diet, so go ahead and enjoy them but in moderation. Health experts say that you should get 30 percent of your total calories from fat.

As calories, fats supply valuable energy to your body. They carry four vitamins—A, D, E, and K—in your blood. Without fat, your body could not use these vitamins. Fats contribute to your body's overall growth and healthy skin. It cushions your vital organs, protecting them from harm. Fat keeps you warm. We have a layer of fat under our skin that insulates us from heat and cold. Finally, fats contribute a lot to enjoyable eating because they taste good and satisfy hunger, since they take longer to digest than proteins or carbohydrates.

Most foods, even many vegetables, contain some fat. But some foods have more fat than others. About 40 percent of our daily fat intake comes from visible fat. That's the fat you see in butter, margarine, vegetable oils, meats, and poultry. But invisible fat makes up the bulk of what we eat; that's the fat in egg yolks, cheese, cream soups, fried foods, chocolate and most desserts, nuts, and seeds.

"What about cholesterol?" asks Vaneeta. "Isn't that fat?" Cholesterol is a fatlike substance, but it is not a fat. That is because it does not supply calories or energy to your body. Cholesterol has a different chemical structure than fat and performs different functions in your body. Your body, specifically the liver, produces enough cholesterol for your needs. Cholesterol also comes from foods and beverages, but only foods of animal origin such as eggs, meat, poultry, fish, and dairy foods. Plants do not produce cholesterol.

Water

What is the body's most important nutrient? Water. Without water, you could not survive for more than a week or so. Although it supplies no calories or energy, every person's cells, tissues, and organs need water to function. Here is why it is so essential: Water keeps your body temperature constant, at about 98.6 degrees Fahrenheit. Heat produced from body processes escapes from your body as water, or sweat, which evaporates on your skin. Water transports nutrients and oxygen to your body cells and carries waste products away. It is the main part of every body fluid, including gastric juices, and it helps prevent constipation by softening stools.

We get most of our water by drinking water and other beverages. You need at least eight cups a day. You also get some water from the foods you eat, usually up to about four cups. If you exercise regularly, do heavy manual work, or live in a hot climate, you may need to drink more water. In general you do not have to worry about drinking too much water, because if you consume more than you need, your body will eliminate the excess. "How can I tell if I'm getting enough water?" Chloe asks. Check your urine. If it is almost clear, you are drinking enough. If it is dark yellow, drink more water.

Nutrition Munchies

"Eat this; don't eat that." Everywhere you turn, whether it's television, radio, newspaper, or the Internet, you hear and see all kinds of nutrition information. Sometimes it is conflicting or confusing. Here are nutrition tips from health experts that will help keep your digestive track running smoothly.

Freshen up your diet. Every day, eat five or more servings of vegetables and fruits. These nutrition power-houses usually contain antioxidants—substances that strengthen the cells in your body and make them better equipped to fight off infections and handle stress. So when you order pizza, top it off with the usual plus a veggie or two. Bagging it? Slip slices of pineapple, apple, pepper, cucumber, carrot, tomato, or zucchini in your sandwich. Pick dips and spreads made with veggies, or add some grated or chopped veggies or fruits to zip up texture, flavor, and nutrition.

Paint your plate. To get the most nutrition from your veggies and fruit, choose deep colors: brilliant reds, dark greens, bright yellows, and oranges. These generally have more nutrients than paler versions.

Do not go hungry. Do not skip meals, especially breakfast and lunch. Maintain your energy level by spreading out your meals. Three meals a day works, or try five or six smaller meals. By not overloading your digestive track, it will work more efficiently.

Avoid quick fixes. Aim for a meal every four to five hours. If you go longer than that, you are more apt to grab convenient foods that are not healthy and are often loaded with salt, sugar, or fat. Snacking is okay. Try a cup of soup, low-fat cereal bars, wheat crackers, yogurt, or fruit.

Thirsty? Grab water, fruit juice, or skim milk. Water has no calories. Fruit juices and skim milk contain essential vitamins and minerals but are not high in calories. Caffeinated beverages—coffee, tea, and many soft drinks—and alcoholic beverages tend to dry out the body because they increase urination. This can lead to constipation.

Snack! But choose high-fiber snacks. Both popcorn and nuts are excellent sources of fiber. Enjoy fruit, especially fruit with edible skins such as apples, pears, peaches, and plums.

Boost your fiber. Just eat one or two whole grains each day along with five servings of vegetables and fruits. Add legumes—dried beans and dried peas—two or three times a week. One way to do this is by eating meatless meals several times a week. So go ahead and have a bean burrito with cheese for lunch or dinner. Make these changes over two to three weeks to give your body time to adjust. Fiber and plenty of water help head off constipation, diarrhea, and other digestive problems.

Say no to dietary supplements—unless your doctor prescribes them. No dietary supplement can fix an ongoing pattern of poor food choices. Only a varied and balanced daily diet provides all the nutrients you need for good overall health. Watch out for bone robbery! If you do not get enough calcium from your daily diet, your body will rob the calcium it needs from your bones. Over time, this can reduce your bone strength and lead to osteoporosis. This potentially crippling disease of thin, fragile bones affects over 28 million Americans according to the National Institutes of Health.

Eat. Devote time just to eating. Do not eat while you are surfing the Internet. Do not eat while you are watching television. Make your mealtimes relaxing. Do not gulp or rush through your food. Slow down and enjoy your meals. You will feel more relaxed, which helps your digestive track work smoothly.

Avoid eating as a way of dealing with problems or handling stress.

Enjoy what you eat. To reduce fat, some teens load up on tasteless, fat-free foods. What happens? They often end up eating too many calories because they are not satisfied. Or they binge later. Either way, this can lead to extra pounds, which puts stress on the digestive system. Instead include a favorite food at every meal. If it's high in fat or sugar, eat just a little; moderation is the key.

Keeping Fit

One of the best-kept secrets of regular exercise is this: It helps keep your digestive system healthy and performing efficiently. It also helps keep your blood circulating and all your systems humming along. When you perform aerobic or "whole-body" exercises, your digestive muscles are toned along with your other muscles. Bending and stretching of your whole body also can add to the health of your digestive tract.

The benefits of exercise do not stop there. Exercise contributes to your overall health because it helps you to be strong, look good, and feel good.

More Benefits

There is even more good news about exercise. Because exercise builds resistance, you are better able to ward off diseases. If you get a cold or the flu, you may restore yourself to health at a faster rate compared to someone who is not fit. Fitness goes hand-in-hand with weight control. Exercise reduces body fat, which means that you are less likely to become overweight.

Chuck says, "After sitting in classes all day, I like to go for a run, play tennis, or walk my dog. If I don't get some exercise during the day, I tire out fast by the evening and find it harder to do my homework."As Chuck discovered, an exercise break refreshes you and gives you an energy boost. And it perks you up for your upcoming activities.

The payoffs of exercise do not stop with the present. Being active now helps reduce your risk of various health problems later on, such as heart disease, obesity, some cancers, and osteoporosis. Osteoporosis is sometimes called the brittle bone disease because the bones are weakened due to a lack of calcium.

One thing that exercise cannot do is overcome a poor diet. You cannot eat a daily diet of high-fat or non-nutritious foods and hope that exercise alone will combat a sluggish digestive system or build strong bones. Exercise and a sound diet together contribute to a healthy you.

Are You Fit?

"I'm in good shape," says Gary. "I run four or five miles most days, and I'm my school's top runner."

Like Gary, Patrice thinks she's fit. "I love basketball, and playing on my school team is lots of fun."

But are these two teens fit? No. Gary can do only about twenty push-ups and fewer chin-ups. He lacks muscle strength. In contrast, Patrice cannot bend over and touch the floor with the palms of her hands. She lacks flexibility, or suppleness.

Being fit is more than being able to run a mile or shoot baskets. Being fit means having the energy and strength to do what you need and want to do in your everyday life. Physical fitness includes five basic parts:

⮞Body composition is the percentage of fat, lean muscle, bone, and water in your body. For teens this translates into using exercise as a means of weight management—to help keep their body fat at a healthy percentage of their total body weight.

⮞Flexibility: You are flexible if you can move a body part through its full range of motion.

⮞ Muscular strength is the ability to exert force against resistance. For example, Melissa is easily able to lift her two-year-old brother off of the floor and onto her shoulders. She can carry lots of sacks of heavy groceries from the car into the kitchen. Her knees, legs, back, and arms have enough strength for her to do these tasks.

⮞Muscular endurance is the ability of your muscles to keep working over a period of time without causing fatigue. Melissa's mother cannot carry more than one or two sacks of groceries into the house without becoming winded. She lacks muscular endurance.

⮞Cardiorespiratory endurance: Both Gary and Patrice have this. Their hearts, lungs, and blood vessels all work together well during long periods of vigorous activity when running or playing basketball.

Get Moving!

Improving your fitness is easier than you think, yet many teens give excuses about why they are physically inactive.

Have you heard any of these? I don't have time. I can't afford the right equipment. I don't like to exercise. I'm too tired to exercise. I'm too fat. None of my friends exercise. I can keep my weight down by watching what I eat.

You may have heard all of these and even some other excuses for not exercising. But they are just that—excuses. The many benefits of exercise make these excuses pretty lame. The great news about being physically active is that you can fit in exercise in many fun ways that all add up to building your strength, endurance, and flexibility.

Not all physical activities give you the same benefits. For example, basketball, running, and tennis strengthen your heart, lungs, and blood vessels. Walking strengthens your leg bones and muscles. To become fit, you need a combination of aerobic, strength-building, and flexibility activities.

Aerobic Activities

In ten seconds, how many aerobic activities can you name? Here are some examples: brisk walking, running, jogging, swimming, dancing, cycling, skating, mopping the floor, climbing stairs, hiking, raking leaves, vacuuming quickly, shooting baskets, playing volleyball or soccer, and jumping rope. During any of these activities, the body increases its demands for oxygen to provide the muscles with energy to carry out the activity.

Aerobic activities typically work the large muscles of the body. In addition, aerobic activities have three things in common:

⮑ They must be brisk or fairly fast to raise the heart and breathing rate.

⮑ They need to be done continuously for at least twenty to thirty minutes without stopping.

⮑ To gain and maintain fitness benefits, you need to do an aerobic activity at least three times a week.

Strength-Building Activities

What comes to mind when you hear *strength-building exercise?* Many people picture a weight lifter bench-pressing some enormous amount. Yet you become a weight lifter whenever you pick up a pile of schoolbooks, carry a bag of heavy groceries, or shovel snow. For each of these activities, you exert a force by using your muscles. The stronger your muscles, the more force you can exert. What this means is that as you continue strength building or weight lifting, your muscle fibers become thicker and can do more work.

To develop strength, choose either or both of these two types of weight-training activities:

⮑ Isometric training involves building muscle strength with little or no movement of the body part. Instead you use muscle tension to build strength. Pushing against a wall is an example.

⮑ Isotonic training involves using weights to make your muscles contract with the movements. This builds muscular strength and flexibility. Calisthenics such as sit-ups, push-ups, and pull-ups are examples of isotonic exercises. Regular lifting of weights, cans, or jugs of water is also isotonic activity.

116

Need help developing a strength-training program? Check out the books and videos at your local library or bookstore. Or head to your YMCA, YWCA, or community center or health center for classes or coaching support.

Stretching Activities

After sitting for hours at a computer or hunched over your homework, do you find yourself stretching your neck from side to side or getting up to stretch your back? Stretching is a natural activity. It feels good because it relieves tension and helps keep your muscles relaxed, which leads to greater flexibility.

Stretching exercises are easy to do and seldom require any equipment. Most stretching exercises take less than two minutes to do from start to finish. Stretching exercises need to be done slowly, just until you feel a slight pull. If you feel pain, you have stretched too much, before your muscles are ready for that level. You will find that the results of stretching become evident quickly. After just a few sessions, you will notice that you can stretch much more easily than before. If you are not sure what kinds of stretching exercises to do or how to do them, your local library or bookstore should carry a variety of books and videos on stretching. Or check out what your YMCA, YWCA, or community center or health center has to offer.

Lifestyle Fitness

Like most people, Sharon says that her life is so hectic that she cannot imagine squeezing in time to exercise each

day. "With school, homework, a part-time job, and practice for the school play, how do I have time to go to a gym
or stick to a workout schedule?"

Many teens can relate to Sharon. However, according
to health and fitness experts, if you sneak in fitness
throughout your day, it will add up to at least thirty minutes of moderate activity during most days. This approach
is sometimes called lifestyle exercising. Although you may
not see the fast, dramatic results of a vigorous aerobic
exercise program combined with weight lifting and
stretching, you will notice positive changes in your
strength, endurance, and flexibility.

The lifestyle approach to exercising is easier than you
might think. For example, instead of getting a ride to her
girlfriend's house, Sharon walks or rides her bike. Each
time, she gets in twenty minutes of aerobic exercise.
When she goes to the mall with her friends, before doing
any shopping, everyone walks briskly once around the
entire mall. In addition to the exercise, Sharon found an
added plus: "I get to scan for any good sales, even in those
places I tend to forget about."

The trick to lifestyle exercising is to learn to think differently. Here are some ideas to get you started: If you usually talk with a friend on the phone for a half hour or so
during the day, try something different. Instead of talking
on the phone, have a conversation while the two of you
go for a walk, cycle, or skate together. If it's raining outside, go ahead and talk on the telephone but also do some
stretching exercises for your neck, shoulders, and back.
Try some muscle strengthening exercises such as arm
curls, side arm raises, calf raises, leg lifts, and leg raises.

Skip the elevator and use the stairs. Do you have favorite television shows that you watch a couple of nights each week? While you are watching television is a great time to do stretching exercises. "I couldn't believe that walking my dog could make such a difference for me," says Lee. "I used to just let her go outside in the backyard. Then I started walking her once in the morning and once in the evening. I discovered that I enjoyed the walks, and I lost five pounds in about a month, just by going for regular walks. I was pleasantly surprised by that!"

You do not need costly equipment or special clothing to do lifestyle exercises. For example, if upper-body muscle strength is an area you want to target, look for opportunities to help yourself—you'll probably get praise from your parents too. Haul out junk from the attic, garage, or basement. Carry dirty clothes downstairs to the washing machine, then carry clean clothes upstairs and put them away. Carry sacks of groceries into the house and put away everything, including cans and heavy items. Shovel snow. You get the idea.

Exercise Ideas Galore

Want to meet new people while getting fit? Join a sports team or an outdoors club. You have plenty to choose from:

- Winter sports: downhill skiing, cross-country skiing, snowshoeing, skating, sledding

- Water sports: swimming, snorkeling, scuba diving, canoeing, kayaking, skiing, surfing, rowing, water aerobics

119

⊸ Racket sports: tennis, racquetball, squash, table tennis, badminton

⊸ Team sports: basketball, soccer, hockey, volleyball, baseball, football, track and field

⊸ Individual sports: dancing, camping, cycling, archery, fencing, in-line skating, horseback riding, mountain climbing, running, golfing, martial arts, and hiking

You probably can add others to this list. Team sports offer a fun way to exercise and to enjoy an activity with a group of people. Your school most likely offers a variety of team sports. Also, see what your community center or place of worship may have available.

"My schedule is so hectic that I prefer to exercise on my own," says Tracy. "I work out with TV exercise shows or videotapes." Other exercise ideas include yoga, walking, running, martial arts, gardening, house cleaning, chopping wood, bicycling, mowing the lawn, and so on. Just move—any kind of movement or physical activity is exercise.

Exercise Programs

Some teens like a well-defined exercise program. Sports teams that meet regularly may fit such exercise requirements. Others prefer to work out by themselves or with a few friends at home or at a gym, health club, or community center.

The first step in starting or improving your exercise program is to set your goals. What do you want to accomplish? Is it strengthening your muscles or becoming more flexible?

Or is it a combination of strength, endurance, and flexibility?

Whatever your goals, find exercises that meet your fitness goals. Choose activities you like to do—you're more likely to stick with them. Also, select several different activities. Variety keeps your exercise routine from becoming dull.

"I like to lift weights and play basketball with my friends a few nights a week," says Darrell. "On weekends we go hiking or cycling. I'm really good about doing all of these activities because they're with my friends, except for weight lifting. That I do by myself. I found that if I do it first thing in the morning, I stick with it. Otherwise, I get so busy with everything else that I forget, and then it's time to go to sleep."

Darrell has hit on a key element of an exercise program: Do it at a regular time during the day or evening. That way it becomes part of your regular routine.

The Three Components

No matter what exercise you enjoy, all exercise programs have three parts: warm-up, workout, and cooldown. During the warm-up, you want to warm up your muscles gradually with slow, smooth movements. Stretching exercises are a great warm-up. So is performing the activity slowly for about five minutes. For example, if you plan to run for thirty minutes, first do a few minutes of slow walking, then a few more of brisk walking.

The workout is when you actually do the exercise—running, for example. During your workout your muscles do a lot of pulling to help you move. This makes them tight and short and, eventually, stronger. To get the greatest benefit from your workout, perform the exercise at least three times a week for twenty to thirty minutes. Build your intensity slowly. If you've never done much running, you may want to run five minutes for the first week. Then go for ten minutes the next week, and so on. By building intensity you are less likely to injure yourself.

After your workout, switch to cooldown. The objective of the cooldown is to allow your body to return to a less active state gradually. The easiest way to do this is to slow down your exercise. So when you are done running, slow to a brisk walk, then to a slower walk. As a final step, do five minutes of stretching to relax muscles that have tightened during your workout. Loose muscles are flexible, move easily, and are less likely to get hurt.

Exercise Pays Off

Remember a couple of exercise tips: Drink plenty of water. Your body loses water when you exercise because you sweat. If you feel any pain while exercising, stop. Exercise should not hurt. You can easily tell the difference between an activity that is exercise and one that is not. Pain is not an essential element of exercise.

Check your exercise program progress by keeping a journal or log sheet. List your goals, then keep track of the frequency, intensity, and duration of the exercise each time you do it. It may take some time, perhaps up to three months, before you notice any major changes or differences. After another three months, compare yourself against where you were when you first started your exercise program. You will be surprised at how much progress you have made.

Managing Stress

"How am I going to get everything done today?"
Susan shook her head.

"What's the problem?" asked her friend Jamie.

"I have to take a math test third period, but I didn't get much studying done. And I let my big biology project go until tonight—it's due tomorrow. But tonight I'm supposed to make dinner, do dishes, and squeeze in my flute lesson after school. My stomach is churning just thinking about all this stress."

Although people use the word "stress" in many ways, stress is how your body and mind react to everyday demands. Stress requires a response from your mind and body, so that you can return to a normal state. Like Susan, many people define stress as something negative. That's called distress, or negative stress. In Susan's case, she is distressed because she has too much to do.

However, stress is not always bad. Some stress can have positive effects. "I get a little nervous before playing another soccer team," says Gene. "Having this kind of positive stress is good for me. It helps me keep alert and focused on playing a good game." Stress can help you achieve your goals, whether studying for a test or performing on stage. Other positive effects of stress include:

⮑ Increased energy level

⮑ Attention to detail

⮑ Feeling excited and hopeful

⮑ Increased self-confidence, motivation, and drive

⮑ Sense of challenge

Another helpful way to look at stress is as a continuum. Too little or too much stress usually is not good over the long term. Too little stress simply may mean that you are not sufficiently motivated, challenged, or stimulated and that as a result your life has become boring. Too much stress means you have too many challenges in your life or that the challenges you face have become so significant that you question your ability to meet them. Somewhere between these two extremes is your stress comfort level, where you feel healthy, motivated, and stimulated.

Stress: The Consequences

Too much stress can do nasty things to your digestive tract and other parts of your body. It tightens your muscles, raises your blood pressure, and zaps your energy. The costs of unchecked stress can really add up. Like Susan, some people react with an upset stomach. Others may have bad breath, insomnia, headaches, and high blood pressure. Your immune system may become weakened, leaving you unable to fight off colds, flu, or other illnesses.

Paul says: "When I'm stressed, I feel anxious and pressured. I can't seem to think as clearly and sometimes can't make up my mind over simple decisions." Mary says that her signal that she's too stressed is fatigue. "I feel tired all the time. I notice that my level of activity goes way down, in school, at home, with my friends. I stop doing fun stuff with my friends, for example. I'm not as mentally sharp and I'm apt to make poor decisions." Loni reacts differently to too much stress. "I get irritable, cynical, and feel down."

We all react differently to stress. However, we generally experience stress in four areas:

- Changes in the body, such as muscle tension and disturbed sleep

- Changes in thinking, such as trouble concentrating and memory lapses

- Changes in emotion, such as feeling blue or angry

- Changes in behavior, such as constant fidgeting or withdrawing from friends

What Is Your Stress Level?

Each of us is comfortable with different levels of stress. Joe likes to be challenged constantly in an ever changing environment. In contrast, Dave prefers a calm atmosphere where things are predictable. Neither situation is better than the other. What is important is to find a balance that works for you: you need enough stress to feel stimulated and energized and you need to be able to manage stress that otherwise would become overwhelming or unhealthy.

How much stress is too much? It depends on the individual; only you can decide that. There are many stress management techniques you can use to learn how to better manage stress in your life and stay at a stress level that is comfortable for you.

Stress Management Techniques

By practicing stress management techniques, you will learn how to make things better for yourself. But learning such skills takes time and practice. You probably will not master all the seven techniques discussed below right away. That is okay because stress will continue to present itself in your life. Since you cannot always control what happens in life, you need to take active control of what you do in response to what life brings you. This is where these stress management skills can help.

Change Your Attitude

Our beliefs or perceptions affect the way we respond to stress. In fact, how we perceive stressful events is a better indicator of how we will respond to stress than the actual events themselves. So if you think about your world in an unreasonable or irrational way, you will feel stressed. What to do? Challenge your unreasonable beliefs.

Imagine that your bedroom has looked the same for as long as you can remember. You are tired of the same old look, but you do not have much money to spend on sprucing things up. What can you do? You can move your furniture around. This will give your room a new look. You can buy one or two items at a garage sale to add something new to your room, perhaps curtains or a waste-basket. Maybe you are really broke, though. How about buying a new frame for that favorite picture you have hanging in there? It is still the same picture, but with the new frame it looks better, fresher.

This same thing applies to your thoughts about stress. If something bothers you and you cannot change it, change how the situation looks by reframing it. That means look-ing at the situation from a different point of view. So if you see something as a threat, look at it instead as a challenge.

Here's an example: You have to give a speech in your history class. If you are like most people, you dislike talk-ing in front of groups, so you may feel anxious and ner-vous. Do not dwell on your negative feelings and thoughts. Instead, think, "I can do this. Kids in my class will want to hear what I have to say. This is interesting information." If you can reframe your thoughts like this, you will feel more confident and self-assured when you get up to talk.

Start tracking whatever inaccurate or unreasonable thoughts you may have that contribute to stress. Some of these include, "I have to be perfect at what I do," or "I can't say 'No' when someone asks me to do something," or "I can't cope." You will often find that thoughts like these are automatic. They pass through the mind quickly, sometimes without you being aware of them. Sometimes these thoughts are in the form of images or memories, not just words.

Once you start to catch your inaccurate or unreasonable thoughts, replace them with more reasonable, balanced thinking. Usually, this type of thinking is more positive. Here are two examples:

Identify Unreasonable/ Inaccurate Thoughts	Challenge Your Thoughts	Reframe or Substitute with Balanced Thinking
I can't cope with this.	I've coped with similar situations before. I can choose what I want to do in this particular situation.	I need some support to get me through this, but I will be fine.
I won't be able to finish my report and it's due tomorrow.	I'll keep calm. I usually get all my assignments in on time, so I know I can do the work.	I'll explain to my teacher tomorrow why I couldn't finish, and ask for a short extension. Or maybe he'll let me turn in what I have done and give me an extension on the rest.

Share Your Feelings

One way to manage stress is to share your feelings with others. Having friends and family members you trust to talk with—your support system—is very helpful. Your support system, though, goes beyond immediate friends and family. It can include other people you trust and respect, perhaps a teacher, counselor, coach, co-worker, etc. A supportive relationship is one in which you feel comfortable sharing your thoughts and feelings.

Having support from others allows you to express feelings of stress and get things off your chest. By talking to others, you often gain a new perspective or a different way of looking at a situation. Supportive people can also help you solidify a determination to take action or can help pull you back to wait until you get more information.

Good, supportive relationships take time to develop. They are created, which means they do not just happen. You need to spend time with the person and let him or her get to know the real you. In turn, you need to be supportive so that the person feels comfortable opening up to you. Support is built on listening and self-disclosure. Learning how much to disclose is a matter of balance—learning when to tell what and to whom.

Be Action-Centered in Living

Ever wake up and think: "I don't feel like getting out of bed so I'm not going to school today?" This is an example of emotion-centered living. Here you are letting your emotions, or the way you feel, govern your actions.

Action-centered living focuses on dealing with your feelings. This includes knowing that:

➯ All feelings have a purpose. Feeling anxious is a warning that you need to prepare. Grief tells you that you have lost something or someone dear to you. When you have a bad feeling such as anger, anxiety, or sadness, ask yourself: "What is this feeling doing in my life?" or "What message is this feeling trying to tell me?" Medicating feelings by overeating or taking drugs, or ignoring bad feelings and stuffing them deep down, will not work for long.

➯ Any feeling, no matter how strong it is right now, will eventually fade and lessen in strength with time. Sometimes this can take minutes, hours, days, or months. The feeling is never constant; sometimes you might feel more grief than at other times, for example.

➯ Your feelings can be influenced by thoughts and actions. Feeling down? Go for a walk or listen to some upbeat music. You may not feel like a walk or listening to music. But do it. Once you move your body or listen to something enjoyable, your attention is distracted from your problem or stressful situation and you'll feel less of the negative emotion.

➯ No matter what you may be feeling, you are responsible for your actions. You may feel angry at your sister for ruining your favorite jeans, but this doesn't mean you have the right to hit her or ruin her favorite jeans. It is all right to acknowledge your feelings by saying to your sister, "I am feeling angry with you because you ruined my jeans."

Sometimes feelings are extremely intense and last a long time. If this happens to you, you may need help from counseling or prescription medication. Most feelings, though, result from living your life fully.

Keep Balanced

People who find a balance in their lives for family, friends, school, and personal needs are better able to manage stress. Balance is an ideal. In reality, balance in your life is in a state of flux. This means trying to achieve balance is an activity you continually engage in as you go through life.

There are five skills that are important in balancing your life:

➩ Try not to overspend your energies. It is all right to say "No" when you're asked to do something for someone else. Recognize your limits and realize that you cannot be everything to everyone.

➩ Know your values and choose commitments consistent with them. Managing stress wisely means spending your time and energy on those things and people that truly matter to you.

➩ Stress management requires that you set boundaries between the different areas of your life: For example, set future goals such as saving enough for a car, and acknowledge current achievements such as celebrating the half-way point of saving for a car.

↪ To maintain balance, periodically look at your life—your achievements, activities, relationships—and evaluate where you want to go—your goals, dreams, and future. This is tough to do, and you may see gaps between what you intend to do and what you end up achieving.

↪ Recharge! Replenish your personal resources by enjoying activities that energize, refresh and refill you. Some ways to recharge include rewarding yourself when you're happy with your work, telling yourself that you are a good person or that you have done a job well, reviewing your goals and perhaps setting new ones, exercising at least every other day, eating nutritional foods, and enjoying a good laugh with your friends each day.

Look Inside Yourself

Observing yourself is another stress-management technique. By looking inward, you become aware of thoughts and concerns that contribute to stress. You will also be more in tune with physical and emotional changes that signal the start of stress.

Each of us has a unique personality. Jenny, say her friends, is warm, nice, and easy to get to know. Her friend Kevin, though, is more reserved and sometimes comes across as a bit standoffish. Katia is confrontational. She's ready to argue with anyone and is never afraid to stand up for her beliefs.

All of us have varying degrees of interpersonal warmth and coolness, passivity and dominance. These differences reflect our personalities. Problems arise when you become fixed and rigid in how you look at and interact with the world. Jenny cannot go through life always being nice to others, if being nice means she is afraid to express anger, disappointment, or to say no. If she does, her self-worth will begin to disappear. She needs to be firm with others at times and look out for her own needs as well as those of others.

When stressed, people tend to become more fixed, more rigid, and more inflexible in the way they think and behave. They tend to become more passive or more dominant, for example. To manage stress, look inside yourself and get to know your interpersonal tendencies—the way you usually act and the way you usually look at the world. Then change what you can to bring out your many different personality traits. For example, do you always eat pepperoni pizza whenever you go out with your friends? Try a veggie pizza next time. Or maybe go to a Greek or Vietnamese restaurant and order something different. Start a new hobby, sport, or activity. Take a different way home and enjoy the scenery.

If you see yourself as a helpless, passive person, redefine yourself as a strong, assertive person, one who can speak up and let your needs be known. The key is to observe your tendencies and then take action to be more flexible and develop your personality.

Take Time to Relax

Reggie says, "My days are so packed, I never have time to relax. I've got too many irons in the fire, as they say, and I have to keep them all going."

Are you like Reggie, with never enough time to kick back and relax? Even in the busiest days, there are times when you can catch a few minutes for yourself. There are many techniques you can use to help you relax such as:

⮕ Practice progressive relaxation. Like most of us, you probably have no idea of the amount of tension you carry in your muscles. You may notice it when you try to relax your sore neck or shoulders after hunching over your homework for an hour or two. If you are aware of the difference between relaxed and tense muscles, you will notice stress sooner and be able to manage it better. To do progressive relaxation, find a comfortable chair to sit or a place to lay down. Close your eyes. Then consciously tense or tighten various muscle groups for five seconds, then let the tension go. Some people start at their toes and work up, while others start from the face down. The muscle groups include: forehead; cheeks and nose; mouth; right and left hand and forearm; right and left biceps; chest and stomach; and right and left thigh, foot and calf, and toes.

⮕ Breathe properly. During stress, you tend to breath more rapidly and your heart rate increases. You breathe more shallowly, so the exchange between fresh oxygen in and waste gases out is not as efficient. Shallow breathing contributes to fatigue, which makes coping with stress harder. To breathe deeply, try to exhale all the gas from your lungs slowly, then breathe in slowly. Expand your abdomen as you breathe deeply. Another way to think of deep breathing is to breathe from your diaphragm instead of taking shallow breaths from your lungs. You can take a few deep, relaxing breaths any time you feel stress coming on. Deep breathing is an instant way to feel more relaxed.

⮑ Exercise. You have already read this elsewhere in this book, but regular exercise is a healthy and effective way to manage stress. It improves your body's well-being and positively affects your mood and the body's digestive and immune systems.

⮑ Eat well. Stress, no matter how well-managed, drains your body of energy. Nourish your body with the nutrients it needs to combat stress and limit foods that aggravate your digestive system.

⮑ Get the amount of rest you need to function well. Teens typically need eight to ten hours of sleep each night.

⮑ Respect your body. Don't smoke, don't drink alcoholic beverages, and don't do drugs.

⮑ Figure out what relaxes you, then make time for at least one thing every day. Some teens find these things relaxing: playing a musical instrument, reading, listening to music, going for a walk, daydreaming, seeing a fun movie, playing with a pet, laughing, and having fun with friends or family. What relaxes you?

Take Responsibility

You cannot always control what causes you stress, but you can control how you react to stress. How you act is up to you. Taking responsibility is learning from past events without being burdened by them. And it is about recognizing that your life constantly brings you fresh moments, both stress-filled and stress-free. When you apply the seven stress management techniques, you'll be better able to handle stressful times and enjoy better overall health.

Getting Help

No one is an expert at handling all of life's challenges and problems. By getting whatever help you need, you can regain your balance and health without unnecessary suffering. Some people may feel uncomfortable with sharing their private thoughts and worries with outsiders, but the benefits really do outweigh whatever uneasiness you might feel. In addition, you get the support you need to make necessary changes.

When should you consider getting outside help? Look for these signs: feeling overwhelmed emotionally, concern about your physical or emotional health, lack of success with your own efforts at resolving problems, or noticing that your suffering is affecting your relationship with family or friends, your work at school, or your participation in other activities. Here are some helpful resources:

➝Community services—some of these resources may be free. To find telephone numbers for these services and hotlines, look in the front pages of your local telephone book or call a public library or hospital.

➝Self-help groups—people facing issues and challenges similar to your own are often a good resource. Alcoholics Anonymous, Al-Anon, Alateen, and Recovery are examples of self-help groups. There are other groups for issues such as grief, time management, drugs, cancer support, and so on. Many of these groups are run by members and are usually free or open to you for a small donation. Check with your local family services and community services organizations to help you find a self-help group. Or your school counselor can help you get in touch with one.

➝See your family care doctor to help you determine if your physical or emotional symptoms are due to causes other than stress. You and your doctor can also decide if medical treatment would be helpful.

➝Psychological counseling can provide you with an in-depth and private focus to help you find solutions to your problems. Counseling is available for individuals or families. Sometimes the costs are covered by a health insurance plan. To find a counselor, ask your family doctor. Or call your local psychology associations, school counselor, or clinical counselor associations.

Glossary

absorption The way nutrients from food move from the small intestine into the cells of the body.

aerobic exercise Vigorous activity that requires the continuous use of oxygen by the body's cells.

allergens Substances that cause the body's immune system to overreact.

antacids Medicines that balance acids and gas in the stomach.

antibiotics Medicines that kill or reduce harmful bacteria in your body.

antibodies Proteins that destroy pathogens in your body.

antidiarrheals Medicines that help control diarrhea.

antispasmodics Medicines that help reduce or stop muscle spasms in the intestines.

anus The opening at the end of the digestive tract,

where feces leaves the body.

barium A chalky liquid used to coat the inside of organs so that they will show up on an X ray.

Barrett's Esophagus Abnormal skin growth on the lower esophagus. It is caused by the presence of cells that normally stay in the stomach lining.

bloating Fullness or swelling in the stomach that can occur after meals.

carbohydrates Sugars, starches, and fibers that are the body's preferred source of energy.

celiac disease Inability to digest and absorb gliadin, the protein found in wheat.

cholesterol A waxy compound present in animal fats that is a necessary chemical component of hormones but also connected with health problems such as arteriosclerosis when found in high levels in the blood.

chronic A symptom or condition that is constant and ongoing.

colitis Irritation of the colon.

computerized axial tomography (CAT scan) An X ray that produces three-dimensional pictures of the body.

constipation Condition in which the stool becomes hard and dry.

Crohn's disease A chronic, or ongoing, form of inflammatory bowel disease.

dietitian An expert in nutrition who helps people plan

what and how much food to eat.

digestion The physical and chemical breakdown of food into smaller pieces.

digestive enzymes Proteins that speed up the breakdown of food.

digestive system The organs in the body that break down and absorb food.

distress Negative stress.

elimination The expulsion of undigested food or body wastes.

endoscope A small, flexible tube with a light and lens on the end. It is used to look into the esophagus, stomach, small intestine, large intestine, or colon. Sigmoidoscope is a type of endoscope.

endoscopy Procedure that uses an endoscope to diagnose or treat a condition.

esophagus The organ that connects the mouth to the stomach.

fatigue A tired feeling that lowers one's level of activity.

fats One of the three main classes of food and a source of energy in the body.

feces Stools.

fiber A substance in food that comes from plants. It helps with digestion by keeping stools soft so that they move smoothly through the colon.

food additives Substances added to food to produce a desired effect such as a certain color or texture.

food allergy A condition in which the body's immune system overreacts to allergens in some foods.

Food and Drug Administration (FDA) A federal agency that ensures all food and food additives, other than meat and poultry, are safe, wholesome and honestly labeled.

foodborne illness A digestive infection caused by food that contains harmful bacteria, usually a result of improper or unhygienic food preparation.

gastric juices Liquids that contain hydrochloric acid, digestive enzymes, and mucus and that start the digestion of proteins.

gastroenterologist A doctor who specializes in digestive diseases.

gastroesophageal reflux disease (GERD) Chronic condition where the flow of the stomach's contents back up into the esophagus.

gluten A protein found in wheat, rye, barley, and oats.

halitosis Bad breath.

H2 blockers Medicines that reduce the amount of acid the stomach produces.

heartburn A painful, burning feeling in the chest, which is caused by stomach acid flowing back into the esophagus.

Heliobactor pylori (H. pylori) A spiral-shaped bacterium found in the stomach that can cause ulcers to form.

hiatal hernia A small opening in the diaphragm that allows the upper part of the stomach to move up into the chest.

hydrochloric acid An acid made in the stomach that breaks down proteins.

immune system The body's defense system for fighting off or protecting against disease.

inflammatory bowel disease (IBD) Long-lasting problems that cause irritation and ulcers in the digestive tract. The most common disorders are ulcerative colitis and Crohn's disease.

insomnia Difficulty or inability to fall asleep or sleep soundly.

intolerance Allergy to a food, drug, or other substance.

irritable bowel syndrome (IBS) A disorder that comes and goes. Nerves that control the muscles in the digestive tract become sensitive to food, stool, gas, and stress.

lactose The sugar found in milk.

lactose intolerance A condition in which the body cannot digest milk sugar.

laxatives Medicines to relieve constipation.

lower esophageal sphincter The muscle between the esophagus and stomach.

magnetic resonance imaging (MRI) A test that takes pictures of the soft tissues in the body.

malnutrition A condition caused by not eating

enough food or not eating a balanced diet.

monosodium glutamate (MSG) A food additive that enhances flavor and is also associated with certain allergic reations.

muscular endurance The ability of muscles to keep working over a period of time without getting fatigued.

nutrients Substances in foods that the body needs to function properly.

pathogens Specific causative agents (viruses or bacteria) that invade the body and attack its cells and tissues, causing many common diseases.

physical fitness The ability to carry out daily tasks easily and have enough reserve energy to respond to unexpected demands.

positive thinking A confident, self-assured way of looking at oneself and the world.

protein One of three main classes of food. It is found in meat, poultry, seafood, eggs, and beans.

protein pump inhibitors Medicines that stop the stomach's acid production.

reflux A condition that occurs when gastric juices or small amounts of food from the stomach flow back into the esophagus and mouth.

stool The solid wastes that pass through the rectum as bowel movements. Also called feces.

stress Mental or physical tension as a response to a condition, situation, or incident.

ulcer A sore on the skin or on the stomach lining usually the result of a baterial infection that eats away at the protective mucus layer of the stomach.

ulcerative colitis Serious disease that causes ulcers and irritation in the inner lining of the colon and rectum.

upper GI series X rays of the esophagus, stomach, and small intestine.

Where To Go for Help

Adler, Joe anne. *Stress: Just Chill Out!* Springfield, NJ: Enslow Publishers, 1997.

American Heart Association. *Fitting in Fitness: Hundreds of Simple Ways to Put More Physical Activity into Your Life.* New York: Times Books, 1997.

Baird, Pat. *Be Good to Your Gut.* Cambridge, MA: Blackwell Science, Inc., 1996.

Balch, James F., and Morton Walker. *Heartburn and What to Do About It.* Garden City Park, NY: Avery Publishing Group, 1998.

Galperin, Anne. *Nutrition.* New York: Chelsea House, 1991.

Janowitz, Henry D. *Good Food for Bad Stomachs.* New York: Oxford University Press, 1997.

Janowitz, Henry D. *Indigestion: Living Better with Upper Intestinal Problems from Heartburn to Ulcers and Gallstones.* New York: Oxford University Press, 1992.

Packard, Gwen K. *Coping with Stress.* New York: Rosen Publishing, 1997.

Peikin, Steven. *Gastro-Intestinal Health*. New York: HarperCollins, 1991.

Reader's Digest. *A Healthy Digestion*. Pleasantville, NY: The Reader's Digest Association, Inc., 1992.

Rosenthal, M. Sara. *The Gastro-Intestinal Sourcebook*. Los Angeles, CA: Lowell House, 1997.

Salter, Charles A. *The Nutrition-Fitness Link: How Diet Can Help Your Body and Mind*. Brookfield, CT: Millbrook Press, 1993.

Schwager, Tina, and Michele Schuerger. *The Right Moves: A Girl's Guide to Getting Fit and Feeling Good*. Minneapolis, MN: Free Spirit Publishing, 1998.

Wolfe, M. Michael, and Thomas Nesi. *The Fire Inside: Extinguishing Heartburn and Related Symptoms*. New York: W. W. Norton & Company, 1996.

For Further Reading

American Academy of Allergy, Asthma, & Immunology
611 E. Wells Street
Milwaukee, WI 53202-3889
(414) 272-6071 or (800) 822-2762
Web site: http://www.aaaai.org

American Allergy Association
P.O. Box 7273
Menlo Park, CA 94026
(415) 322-1663

American College of Gastroenterology
4900 B South 31 Street
Arlington, VA 22206
(703) 820-7400
Web site: http://www.acg.gi.org/

American Gastroentrological Association
7910 Woodmont Avenue, 7th Floor
Bethesda, MD 20814
(301) 654-2055
Web site: http://www.gastro.org/

Celiac Disease Foundation
13251 Ventura Boulevard, Suite 3
Studio City, CA 91604
(818) 990-2379

Celiac Sprue Association/United States of America, Inc.
P.O. Box 31700
Omaha, NE 68131-0700
(402) 558-0600

Crohn's & Colitis Foundation of America, Inc.
386 Park Avenue South, 17th Floor
New York City, NY 10016-8804
(800) 932-2423 or (212) 685-3440
Web site: http://www.ccfa.org

Cyclic Vomiting Syndrome Association
13180 Caroline Court
Elm Grove, WI 53122
(414) 784-6842
Web site: http://www.beaker.iupui.edu/cvsa

Food Allergy Network
10400 Eaton Place, Suite 107
Fairfax, VA 22030-2208
(703) 691-3179 or (800) 929-4040
Web site: http://www.foodallergy.org

Gluten Intolerance Group of North America
P.O. Box 23053
Seattle, WA 98102-0353
(206) 325-6980

International Foundation for Functional Gastrointestinal
   Disorders
P.O. Box 17864
Milwaukee, WI 53217
(888) 964-2001 or (414) 964-1799
Web site: http://www.execpc.com/iffgd

Intestinal Disease Foundation, Inc.
1323 Forbes Avenue, Suite 200
Pittsburgh, PA 15219
(412) 261-5888

National Center for Nutrition and Dietetics of the American
    Dietetic Association
216 West Jackson Blvd., Suite 800
Chicago, IL 60606-6995
(800) 366-1655 or (900) 225-5267
Web site: http://www.eatright.org

National Digestive Diseases Information Clearinghouse
2 Information Way
Bethesda, MD 20892-3570
(301) 654-3810
Web site: http://www.niddk.nih.gov

National Organization for Rare Disorders, Inc.
P.O. Box 8923
New Fairfield, CT 06812-8923
(800) 999-6673 or (203) 746-6518
Web site: http://www.NORD-RDB.com/~orphan

Pediatric/Adolescent Gastroesophageal Reflux Association,
    Inc.
P.O. Box 1153
Germantown, MD 20875-1153
(301) 601-9541
Web site: http://www.reflux.org

Index

A

absorption, 8, 18, 24, 63, 74-75, 78, 103
adrenaline, 97
Africa, 76
alcohol, 12, 22, 25, 27, 29, 34, 40, 43, 44-45, 65, 110
allergens, 84
American Board of Allergy and Immunology, 90
anaphylactic reaction/shock, 62, 89-90, 96-97
anaphylaxis, 85, 89-90
anemia, 77
antacids, 41-42, 47, 60
antibiotics, 24, 57-59
antidepressants, 31
antihistamines, 34, 91, 94
antioxidants, 109
antispasmodics, 26, 31
artificial fats, 24, 29
aspirin, 45, 54
asthma, 65
attitude, 126-128

B

bacteria, 9, 16, 18, 20, 24-26, 54-60, 62, 64, 65, 70, 72, 104
bad breath, 15, 20-21, 52
Barrett's esophagus, 37, 48-50
belching and burping, 18, 19, 24
biotin, 105
bloating, 5, 15, 18, 21, 27, 52, 62, 63, 68, 77, 88

C

caffeine, 22, 25, 27, 29, 66, 110
calcium, 101, 104, 111, 113
cancer, 2, 12, 28, 37, 49-50, 54, 78, 104,113
carbohydrates, 16, 18, 100, 106-107
carbonated beverages/soft drinks, 19, 22, 29, 45, 110
celiac disease, 74-82
China, 76
chloride,101
chocolate, 27, 40, 43, 45, 66, 95
cholesterol, 108
chromium, 102

citrus, 43, 45
coffee, 22, 40, 43, 45, 110
colitis, 26, 28
computerized axial
    tomography (CAT)
    scan, 13-14
constipation, 4, 5, 21-24, 27,
    31, 88, 100, 106, 109,
    110, 111
copper, 102
counseling and other help,
    136-137
Crohn's disease, 28
cross-reactivity, 86
cryptosporidium, 24

D

diarrhea, 4-5, 24-26, 27, 41,
    58, 62-63, 65, 68, 77,
    88, 100, 106, 111
diet, 12, 22, 28, 29, 81, 99-
    100, 109
diary, 91-92
digestion, 2-3, 8, 84, 99-111
digestive diseases, 2, 11-15,
    68, 75
digestive disorders, 26
digestive system, 4-8, 72, 87,
    88, 99
  explanation of, 5-7
  how it works, 8
  length, 6
dizziness, 32, 58
doctors
  choosing, 14-15
  getting help from, 12-14
drugs

over-the-counter (OTC), 2,
    15, 19, 22, 23, 25, 41-
    42
prescription, 12, 23, 28,
    46, 57, 74

E

E coli, 24
endoscopes, 13, 79
endoscopic exams, 13, 47-
    48, 50, 56, 79
epinephrine, 97
esophagitis, 37
esophagus, 6, 36, 40, 44, 47-
    48
exercise, 12, 23, 29, 112-122
  aerobic activities, 115-116
  lifestyle activities, 117-119
  strength-building, 116-117
  stretching exercises, 117

F

fats, 100,.107-108
fever, 25, 26, 28
fiber, 16-17, 22, 29, 100,
    106, 110-111
supplements, 31
fitness, 99, 112-122
flatulence, 18
flu, 24
fluorine, 102
folic acid, 105
food
  additives, 64-66, 86
  allergies, 83-98
  high fat, 19, 25, 29, 43,
    45, 99

intolerances, 5, 61-82, 84, 87
poisoning, 24, 62, 65, 84
sensitivities, 62-63
spicy, 45, 54
Food and Drug Administration (FDA), 64, 65-66, 86, 95
fructose, 17, 29, 67
fruits, 17, 22, 25, 26, 45, 81, 99, 106, 109-111

G
garlic, 45
gas, 5, 16-20, 27, 62, 63, 68, 77
gastritis, 5
gastroenteritis, 12
gastroesophageal reflux disease (GERD), 4, 18, 36-50, 52
gastrointestinal (GI) system, 4, 6
gastrointestinal tests, 13, 47, 56
giardiasis, 24
gluten, 62, 63-64, 74-82
intolerance, 75-82
gum disease, 21

H
heartburn, 4, 35-50, 52
hiatal hernia, 39-40
histamine, 66, 84
H. Pylori, 55-60
H2 blockers, 41, 46, 57-58, 60

hunger, 9, 20-21, 110
hydrochloric acid, 7, 9
hyperactivity, 67

I
ibuprofen, 54
immune system, 62, 79, 84, 98
indigestion, 2-3
infection, 11-12, 54-56, 109
intestines, 6, 7, 12, 16, 18, 26. 28. 47, 63, 68, 70, 74-75, 80, 104
iodine, 102-103
Ireland, 76
iron, 103
irritable bowel syndrome (IBS), 5, 26-31

L
lactose, 17, 29, 63-64, 67-74
lactose intolerace, 61-62, 64, 67-74, 87
laparoscope, 49
laxatives, 22, 23, 31
lifestyle changes, 28, 42-44

M
magnesium, 101
magnetic resonance imaging (MRI), 14
malnutrition, 78
manganese, 103
metabolism, 5, 63, 103
milk products, 17, 27, 29, 43, 62, 67-74, 85-86
minerals, 100-103
mints, 43, 45, 89, 106

molybdenum, 103
monosodium glutamate (MSG),
    64, 65-66, 82, 86
motion sickness, 32-34
mouth, 6, 88
mucosa, 5, 9
mustard, 45

N
National Food Allergy
    Network, 89
National Institute of Allergy
    and Infectious
    Diseases, 83
National Institute of Diabetes
    and Digestive and
    Kidney Diseases, 4,
    38, 55, 76
National Institutes of Health,
    2, 27, 54, 55, 68, 98,
    111
nausea, 2, 24, 25, 32, 52, 58,
    63, 66, 68, 88
niacin, 105
nonsteroidal anti-
    inflammatory agents
    (NSAIDs), 54, 59-60
nutrients, 100, 111

O
obesity, 40, 44, 113
onions, 45
osteoporosis, 78, 111, 113
overeating, 30

P
panthothenic acid, 105

peristalsis, 6
phosphorus, 101-102, 104
potassium, 25, 102
pregnant women, 39, 40, 78
proteins, 100, 107
proton-pump inhibitor, 46,
    57-58, 60
protozoa, 24, 26

R
relaxation, 12, 30, 133-135

S
salmonella, 25
screening tests, 12
selenium, 103
shock, 24, 63, 65
sigmoidoscope, 13, 28
skin tests, 92-93
smoking, 11-12, 19, 29, 33,
    40, 44, 58-59
sodium, 25, 102
sorbital, 17, 29
spastic colon, 26
sphincter muscle, 6, 36, 39,
    44, 49
starches, 16-17, 106
stomach, 6-7, 28, 36, 47
    common problems, 3-5,
        11-34
    juices, 7, 20, 44
    upset, 1-2, 4, 15, 62
stress/stress management, 24,
    27, 28, 30, 40, 54,
    123-127
sugars, 5, 16-17, 22, 54, 66,
    106

sulfites, 65, 86
support systems, 129
surgery, 12, 48-49, 60

T
tomato products, 42, 45
tranquilizers, 31, 33
traveling, problems when, 23,
    24, 32-34

U
ulcerative colitis, 28
ulcers, 2, 4, 18, 37, 51-60
ultrasound, 13
U.S. statistics, 2, 4, 5, 25, 27,
    51, 55, 68, 69, 76, 83

V
vegetables, 17, 22, 26, 81,
    99, 106, 108, 109-111
vinegar, 45
vitamins, 100, 103-106

vitamin A, 104, 107
vitamin B, 104-105
vitamin C, 106
vitamin D, 103-104, 107
vitamin E, 104, 107
vitamin K, 103-104, 107
vomiting, 4, 5, 15, 26, 32,
    39, 52-53, 58

W
water, 100, 108-109
    drinking enough, 22,
    25, 30, 31, 111, 122

X
X rays, 14, 47, 56

Z
zinc, 103

St. Margaret Middle School Library
1716-A Churchville Road
Bel Air, Maryland 21015